how to
WRITE
your WILL

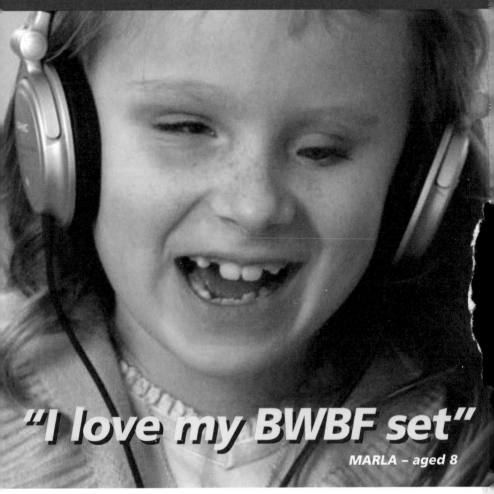

Remember me...

Fatmata Sesay,
8 years old, Nyandehun
Village, Sierra Leone

Photo: Liba Taylor/ActionAid

Can you find a place for a poor child in your Will?

By remembering ActionAid in your Will, you can help transform the lives of poor children and their families.

ActionAid is one of the UK's leading overseas development charities and has been working with poor communities for over 35 years. Last year alone, we reached more than 13 million people. Please help us continue our work for as long as it's needed.

Whether large or small, a gift in your Will could leave the world a better place for countless poor children and their families. It could give them access to clean water, sufficient food or the chance to go to school.

Call now on **020 7561 7668,** email **legacy@actionaid.org.uk** or **visit www.actionaid.org.uk**

how to
WRITE
your WILL

The complete guide to structuring
your will, inheritance tax planning,
probate and administering an estate

19th edition

Marlene Garsia

KOGAN
PAGE

Readers should check before taking irrevocable action in case of changes to the law.

While every care has been taken to ensure the accuracy of the contents of this work, no responsibility for loss occasioned to any person acting or refraining from action as a result of any statement in it can be accepted by the Author. Amendments have been made following the Chancellor's Budget Statement on 22 April 2009. Readers should be aware of this and obtain details of any late amendments.

First published in 1989 entitled *How to Write a Will and Gain Probate*
Thirteenth edition 2003 entitled *How to Write Your Will*
Fourteenth edition 2004
Fifteenth edition 2006
Sixteenth edition 2007
Seventeenth edition 2008
Eighteenth edition 2009
Nineteenth edition 2009

Kogan Page Limited
120 Pentonville Road
London N1 9JN
United Kingdom
www.koganpage.com

British Library Cataloguing in Publication Data

A CIP record for this book is available from the British Library.

ISBN 978 0 7494 5540 8

Typeset by Saxon Graphics Ltd, Derby
Printed and bound in Great Britain by Thanet Press Ltd, Margate

Give a retired Greyhound the WILL to live.

There's a hopeful, trusting look in the eyes of most retired greyhounds. They're hoping for a comfortable retirement home and they trust us to provide it for them!

How can you help? With the best will in the world, you may not be able to either adopt or sponsor a greyhound right now. But a legacy could be the answer. For example, a tax-effective way of donating is to remember us in you will. You could consult your solicitor when drawing up your will to ensure that your money goes where you decide. For more information on how to leave a legacy to the Retired Greyhound Trust, email or phone us on: **0844 826 8424**

Retired Greyhound Trust
2nd Floor, Park House, 1-4 Park Terrace,
Worcester Park, Surrey KT4 7JZ
greyhounds@retiredgreyhounds.co.uk
www.retiredgreyhounds.co.uk

retired greyhound trust

Charity No. 269668

PLANTS PEOPLE
POSSIBILITIES

A legacy to Kew is a gift for life

We don't only protect rare plants at Kew, we are also trying to conserve a world worth living in for generations to come. After all, we rely on plants for the very air that we breathe.

Kew's work includes the conservation of rare plant species, research into plant uses, and education for all ages, as well as the care of the world famous Gardens for the enjoyment of many thousands of visitors each year.

Legacies are vital to the future of Kew, and are an essential source of support for Kew's mission to inspire and deliver science-based plant conservation worldwide, enhancing the quality of life.

For further information, and a free copy of our legacy booklet, please contact:

Legacy Department, Foundation and Friends, Royal Botanic Gardens, Kew
FREEPOST, Richmond, Surrey TW9 1BR

Telephone: 020 8332 3249   E-mail: legacies@kew.org
Fax: 020 8332 3201   Web: www.kew.org

Registered Charity Number: 803428

The Purcell School

FOR YOUNG MUSICIANS

Royal Patron: HRH The Prince of Wales
President: Sir Simon Rattle

Remembering the Purcell School in your will is a wonderful way to continue your support for a cause close to your heart.

The Purcell School mission is to provide young musicians of exceptional promise and talent with the best possible teaching and environment in which to fulfil their potential, irrespective of their background.

Leaving a legacy to the School is one of the most enduring gifts you can make and is an investment for future generations of young musicians.

For more information on how you can help by leaving a legacy to the Purcell School, please visit www.purcell-school.org or call us on 01923 331100

Registered Charity No 312855

The Purcell School for young musicians

Established in 1962, the Purcell School was the first specialist music school in the UK. It is a founding member of the Government's Music and Dance Scheme that was set up to ensure that exceptionally gifted children could receive suitable training and education from an early age.

The School is co-educational and takes young musicians between the ages of 9 and 18 and has been awarded UNESCO's Mozart Gold Medal 'in recognition of its unique contribution to music, education and international culture'. It has gained a worldwide reputation as a centre of excellence.

Entry to the School is by audition and it is central to our philosophy that no pupil worthy of a place should be denied it due to their personal financial circumstances. In spite of the widely held misconception that classical music and music making is a preserve of the wealthy, almost every child receives some degree of financial support.

We are also sympathetic to the needs of children who started out with adequate private funding in place but whose family's finances later take a dramatic turn for the worse. In these instances, we do all we can to ensure the pupil's education continues uninterrupted. Not surprisingly perhaps, in recent times we have seen an increasing number of requests for help placed upon our limited resources.

The support of generous donors is essential if we are to continue to provide the very best young musicians in the land with the education and training they deserve.

Please help us give an outstanding musical education to as many gifted children as possible by leaving a legacy to the Purcell School.

Registered Charity No.312855

Please help us...

to provide tennis-playing opportunities for children and adults with disabilities

The Dan Maskell Tennis Trust raises funds to support tennis for the disabled in three main areas wheelchair, deaf and learning disabilities.

The Trust provides specialist wheelchairs, tennis equipment and grants towards court hire and coaching for individuals, clubs and disability organisations.

A specialist chair costs £2,000, a bag of equipment £250 and our maximum grant is £1,000. We need donations and legacies to help the ever-increasing number of disabled players fulfill their potential.

THANK YOU

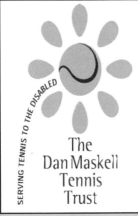

SERVING TENNIS TO THE DISABLED

The Dan Maskell Tennis Trust

The Dan Maskell Tennis Trust,
c/o The Tennis Foundation,
The National Tennis Centre,
100 Priory Lane, Roehampton,
London SW15 5JQ

Tel 020 8487 7119
Email dmtt@tennisfoundation.org.uk
Web: www.danmaskelltennistrust.org.uk

Part of the Tennis Foundation registered charity no. 298175

Contents

Acknowledgements

I would like to thank all those who have helped me in writing this book, and in particular Chris Marsh, former Registrar, who has always been helpful and constructive with his comments when reading this text; HMRC Helpline; Scottish Courts library section; and Hills and Co.

What better gift could you give than the gift of life?

The Institute of Cancer Research is one of the world's leading cancer research organisations and is internationally renowned for the quality of its science.

By leaving a gift in your Will to The Institute, you can help our scientists to reach the ultimate goal that one day people may live their lives free from the fear of cancer as a life-threatening disease.

The Institute of Cancer Research was founded in 1909 to investigate the causes, diagnosis and treatment of cancer. With 850 scientists on its two sites on the Fulham Road in central London and at Sutton in Surrey, it ranks today as one of the world's top four cancer research centres and it is the only one of these outside the USA. Its internationally leading research into genetics, molecular biology and drug development is unrivalled anywhere in the world.

In 2009 we celebrate our Centenary. Over the years, *we have grown to become one of the largest cancer research foundations in the world, the best in Europe and a global leader in developing treatments and in controlling the disease.*

The Institute of Cancer Research discoveries have not only fuelled its own continuing research but also informed and influenced other discoveries at other institutions around the world.

Some of our Achievements :

1910 – The Institute of Cancer Research founds a specialist radiotherapy department – one of the first in the world

1930s – The Institute of Cancer Research identifies the suspected link between smoking and lung cancer.

1950s – The Institute of Cancer Research develops the drugs busulphan, chlorambucil and melphalan – all of them outstandingly successful in treating cancer and which are still used today.

1960s – The Institute of Cancer Research scientists show that carcinogens act by damaging DNA, leading to the dramatic discovery that the basic cause of cancer is a DNA malfunction.

1970s – The Institute of Cancer Research develops carboplatin, the use of which becomes the global standard of care for patients with a wide range of solid tumours, and leads to the high cure rate for testicular cancer.

1995 – The Institute of Cancer Research identifies the breast cancer gene BRCA2, mutations in which predispose carriers to high risk of breast cancer. The finding provides the opportunity to initiate breast cancer prevention studies.

2000 – The Institute of Cancer Research scientists initiate the Cancer Genome Project with the aim of identifying genes that have relevance to particular cancers. The project, being conducted at the Wellcome Trust's Sanger Institute, has so far discovered over 350 genes associated with cancer.

You could help make our first centenary our last by remembering The Institute of Cancer Research in your Will. Your Legacy could save lives.

Making a Will is perhaps more important than you think, because if you die without one then everything does not automatically pass to your partner or spouse. Making a Will is easy and by doing so you can make sure that all your wishes are fully reflected within the document. You may think that there is no need to write a Will because you do not have very much to leave. Make a list of your assets and you will be surprised at how much you do have. You can use your Will to leave a gift to a charity such as The Institute of Cancer Research. People often chose to do this as they are not in the position to donate to charity during there lifetime. By leaving a gift to The Institute of Cancer Research in your Will, you could help fund our ground breaking work and save lives. Making a Will does not take much time, but its effects are long-lasting and far-reaching.

Remember that any gift you leave to charity in your Will are exempt from Inheritance Tax, so the tax burden on your estate is reduced.

Here at The Institute of Cancer Research we offer a Will for Free scheme where you can receive independent, professional advise allowing you to make a basic Will or update an existing one for free using one of your local participating solicitors.*

We make this offer in the hope that you could help fund our vital research although you are under no obligation to do so and providing for your family and friends must of course take priorty.

We would be delighted if you could support our work by leaving a legacy to The Institute of Cancer Research. However, to ensure that your intended gift is received your solicitor must ensure that our full details are specified correctly within your Will.

The Institute of Cancer Research
123 Old Brompton Road
London
SW7 3RP

X 90004 – Charity exemption number

For more information about The Institute of Cancer Research or further legacy Information, please contact us on : 0207 153 5387 or E-mail legacy@icr.ac.uk

Preface

Despite ongoing publicity encouraging individuals to make wills, the majority of people still do not do so. The reasons given are many and varied. But it means that thousands of letters of administration are issued each year to relatives or friends of the deceased, simply because the deceased failed to make a will.

It may be that a visit to a solicitor is thought costly, which at present it is not. For solicitors often do deals whereby wills can be made for £120 a person, well below their normal charge-out rates, and sometimes it can even be done free of charge by using a charity's contract. However, should a solicitor be named as an executor their normal hourly charge would apply and this would be more expensive unless you negotiate a fixed price for dealing with probate. Using a solicitor does not mean that all matters will go smoothly and that the wording in the will will be without dispute. There have been occasions when the wording in a will completed by a solicitor has been such that it has caused a dispute.

You do not, however, have to seek professional help. A 'Do-It-Yourself' approach, provided it is done carefully, can quite adequately be carried out by an inexperienced person. This applies both to writing your will and to dealing with probate matters for a deceased relative or friend. Indeed, if you are the residuary beneficiary of a will, it would also be more profitable to deal with the probate yourself through the Personal

Applications Department of your nearest Probate Registry, than to pay professional charges, which start at £140 per hour but can be £180 per hour plus VAT, sometimes more. A 'Do-It-Yourself' approach has many benefits, as you will see as you read this book. But it will prove very difficult emotionally should you be proving the estate of a partner or loved one. For this reason, you would be well advised to consider using the services of a solicitor or to rely on a fellow executor.

This book has been written for most people, from those who want to know but do not know whom to ask to those who still have questions, perhaps simply about the value of their estate. It has been written by a layperson for a layperson. And it has been written in plain English with as little use of legalistic words and phrases as the text will allow. The book is a practical and basic guide on how to write a will and gain probate. After all, it is a subject that touches all our lives at some time.

I have started at the very beginning, with what I would have to do myself when writing a will and working on from that point.

This book has been written sequentially, step by step, so that readers can clearly follow what to do next whether writing their own will, planning their estate or acting as executors carrying out their obligations on behalf of a deceased friend or relative. Alternatively, the layout of the book allows readers to dip in at the spot appropriate to their questions and needs. Frequently asked questions are answered. How do you write your own will? What makes a will invalid? Who can be called upon to deal with an estate? Where do you find your nearest Probate Registry? What happens if you die without making a will? What the text does not cover is dealing with disputes or contesting a will. Should this happen, then you should seek the advice of a solicitor and perhaps seek a barrister's opinion. What this book does is point out areas of potential problems, but as readers can appreciate, it cannot cover all detail and cases as they are potentially so numerous. Legal advice in these instances is recommended.

In researching this book it has become clear that, under English law, provided an estate is relatively straightforward, complicated trusts are not involved, and extensive estate planning is not needed, then there is nothing to stop the individual from handling his or her relation's or friend's affairs – whatever the size of the estate. Despite this, only a minority of people do so.

Scotland is another matter. I have explained briefly the position in Scotland, dealing with small estates, the differences when writing a will and gaining Confirmation. The information given is not exhaustive since in Scotland solicitors' help is often required by the authorities. The level of assistance is not available to the same degree as that found in England and Wales, nor do matters appear as straightforward – except for processing small estates.

The appropriate authorities in both England and Scotland have been extremely helpful, as they would be to any person seeking their assistance. There are significant changes under way not only with new laws but a change in the probate system and updating of excepted estates. Capital Taxes Office have introduced a call centre processing system although the initial contact is still to be made with your local Probate Registry. A proposed simplification in dealing with the Registries has been introduced. As an executor or proposed administrator you have to present yourself to the Registrar and swear that the information given is correct; in future 'a statement of truth' will replace the oath, although personal attendance will still be necessary. Some changes affect legal status in the form of civil partnerships. For example, a bill allows same sex partners who died intestate to have their surviving civil partner named as administrator of the estate and to receive assets from the estate as if they had been married. This includes the benefit of nil inheritance tax on transfer of assets.

Family responsibilities necessitate family and financial decisions. How do you best ensure that your children's inheritance is not taken away by the Treasury? What options are available when arranging your affairs? Is insurance the answer?

In his March 2006 Budget, the Chancellor proposed radical changes to the tax regime on trusts. In particular, accumulation and maintenance and discretionary trusts were hit the hardest, with some 'interest in possession' trusts and insurance-based policies/trusts also requiring change. The Treasury estimated that only £15 million would be gained in tax by these measures, but professional advisers estimate that the figure is closer to £200,000 million. It appears that the professional advisers' figures will be the closest. Moreover, Chancellor Darling, in his 22 April 2009 Budget, announced a further increase in tax on discretionary trust up from 40 per cent to 50 per cent.

On 9 October 2007 the Chancellor announced changes to the Inheritance Tax (IHT) threshold affecting married couples or civil partners. What he did was to allow the transfer of the unused nil rate of inheritance tax on the first partner's death at the rate applicable on the second spouse's death. This applies from November 2007. The IHT threshold as applicable at the time of the first death no longer matters. However, this tax treatment can only apply if no previous tax planning has been done on the first death and, importantly, it only applies to married or civil partners so single people or those living together outside of marriage or civil partnership do not benefit. The rate of IHT has marginally increased from £312,000 in 2008/09 to £325,000 in 2009/10.

Tax changes for those who are not UK domiciled were also presented in the 2008 Budget. Any readers affected by these changes should take professional advice.

The readers who use this book will find it helpful in all relevant aspects. It is not meant as a definitive book on all subjects covered where all possible questions are asked and answered as that would require volumes of text and pages and a number of experts in different subjects. However, you can take heart, as you will find no unexplained text to baffle you, merely straightforward information as to what needs to be done and how to do it.

The Friends of The Wisdom Hospice

Partners in Care

The Wisdom Hospice provides specialist palliative care for people throughout Medway and Swale with terminal illnesses. This is provided through in-patient care, Day Hospice or under the care of the Domiciliary Nursing Team.
Around 900 patients and their families benefit from this service each year.
Approximately 30% of the total running costs are met by
The Friends of the Wisdom Hospice.

For further information please contact:
Caroline Ford,
Administrator/Fundraising Manager
The Friends of the Wisdom Hospice,
High Bank, St Williams Way,
Rochester, Kent ME1 2NU
Phone: 01634 831163 Fax: 01634 849975
E-mail: info@friendsofthewisdomhospice.org.uk

The Wisdom Hospice was opened in 1984 and was named after Molly Wisdom who raised money for a hospice in the Medway area, even though she herself was dying of cancer. Following her example the Friends of The Wisdom Hospice were able to raise the rest of the funds to build the Hospice.

The Wisdom Hospice is now run by the Palliative Care Services of NHS Medway Primary Care Trust. The Hospice provides specialist palliative care for patients throughout Medway and Swale with terminal illnesses.

The Friends of The Wisdom Hospice make an annual grant to the Medway PCT of £502,000 towards the running costs of the Hospice. Additional funds have been made available for increased staffing.

In addition the Friends fund the hairdressing service and chaplaincy at the Hospice and provide extra equipment and facilities that do not fall within the PCT budget. To provide extra care for patients in their own homes, annual grants are made by the Friends to Crossroads and the Marie Curie Nursing Service.

The Friends of the Wisdom Hospice relies on the support of the community to maintain and extend the services provided. Income from legacies is vital to allow us to continue this level of support. We need to raise in excess of £2000 each and every day.

Over the past few years income from legacies has help us to fund a £1.5m extension and refurbishment project at the Hospice and to landscape the patio garden to provide extra comfort and privacy for patients and their families.

Please consider leaving a gift in your Will to the Friends of The Wisdom Hospice to enable our work to continue in support of people with life limiting conditions throughout Medway and Swale.

BKPA *Legacy Appeal*

No amount of money can free *Tai* from a lifetime on dialysis.

Only a successful transplant can do this.

In the meantime the British Kidney Patient Association strives to improve the quality of life for kidney patients and their families throughout the UK.

Legacies will really make a difference to our ongoing work.
To find out more about the BKPA please visit www.britishkidney-pa.co.uk
or call us on 01420 472021

BRITISH KIDNEY
Patient ASSOCIATION
improving life for kidney patients

The British Kidney Patient Association

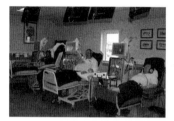 

The BKPA is a well established charity working to improve the quality of life for adults and children in the UK with kidney disease.

- We provide information, support and advice to individuals and their families.

- We give grants to help patients and families in financial difficulty cover the costs of domestic bills, hospital travel and education.

- Our grants also help adults and children take short breaks and holidays when they are otherwise unable to go, and we fund activity holidays for children and staff from children's kidney centres.

- In addition, we provide financial support to kidney units throughout the UK for initiatives that will improve the quality of service and care, which are not covered by the NHS.

Everything we do is focussed on improving daily life for kidney patients. Life with kidney disease can be mentally and physically demanding; patients have to cope with changes in their health, numerous hospital visits, the effects on work and family life and associated financial issues. Patients need our support.

The British Kidney Patient Association
BKPA
Bordon
Hampshire
GU35 9JZ
Tel 01420 472021
www.britishkidney-pa.co.uk
A Charitable Company limited by Guarantee No 270288

We look forward to hearing from you

This has not always been easy. Following the decline of the use of horses in industry, transport and agriculture, with the rise of the motor vehicle and the mechanisation of farming, things seemed bleak for the Shire, and in the 1960's the Society had to take drastic action to reverse the falling numbers of Shires. They have done this with great vigour and now the future of the breed looks good. A resurgence of interest in Shire Horses as both leisure animals and environmentally friendly transport has led to an increase in breeding numbers.

However, the Society is never complacent and there is always more work to do. The Society is constantly working to maintain high breed standards. Stallion inspections are mandatory before full registration in the Stud book.

The Society is also keen to promote awareness of the Shire's history and future with the general public. The Society runs the Shire Horse Centre at Sacrewell Farm and Country Centre, where you can interact with and learn more about these gentle giants. There are also courses run at the centre and special events, including demonstrations of working Shires.

The Shire Horse Society holds its Spring Show at the East of England Showground every March. The Show is the largest gathering of Shire Horses in the Country. The Society also organises the Shire Horse of the Year Show.

To find out more about the Shire Horse Society please contact 01733 234451 or visit the website www.shire-horse.org.uk.

Autism touches everyone. Where does it touch you?

Autism is not rare. In the UK alone, there is an estimate of over **500,000** individuals with autistic spectrum disorders. This condition has huge implications for their lives and the lives of their families... and yet...

...very little is known about the best ways of helping these people.

Research is desperately needed, and you can help...

If you would consider a legacy, please call 07866 074528 or go to www.researchautism.net

RESEARCH AUTISM
IMPROVING THE QUALITY OF LIFE

Research Autism
Registered Charity No. 1096508

"After our son was diagnosed we would literally try everything we could lay our hands on that promised to help. We followed up leads from the internet and popular press and it seemed that many of the professionals were as much in the dark as we were. We now know that many of the things on offer were a waste of time; some little more than 'snake oil treatments'."

Alex, parent of six-year-old Shaun.

Alex is just one out of the 540,000 people with autism in the UK.

What is autism and how does it affect people?

The term "autism spectrum" describes a range of neurodevelopmental conditions, usually present from early childhood and persisting through life, which are associated with difficulties in social functioning, communication and behaviour.

Without timely and informed help and support, there can be potentially devastating consequences for the person concerned and those around them. These may include extreme anxiety and distress, injury, withdrawal and exclusion. Those affected require individualised services and support throughout their lives. Without such support they are vulnerable and likely to lead stressful, socially isolated and disadvantaged lives.

Did you know?
- Autism covers a wide spectrum of people with very different needs
- Over half of people with autism are of normal or above-average I.Q.
- Only 15% of adults with autism are in full-time employment

The desperate need for research

Despite the large number of people affected by autism, and the severe implications on their lives, very little is known about the best ways of helping them.

We need to learn much more about the effects of the various interventions and therapies and which is most likely to be effective with a particular individual.

Without impartial information and sound advice, parents may be seduced by claims for treatments and other approaches potentially misleading or exaggerated. They need confidence that the methods they choose are based on sound scientific principles.

Please show a deafblind child that they are not alone

For children who are both deaf and blind, the world can be a lonely and frightening place. But with your support, there's so much we can do to help.

Sense is a pioneering charity in the UK offering lifelong support, advice, education and practical help to deafblind children and adults – and their families. By leaving a gift to Sense in your Will, you could turn a lifetime of isolation into an amazing world of hope and discovery.

For further information about leaving a legacy to Sense, please call, email or write to us (quoting LAD204), at the address below.

Legacies Department, Sense
101 Pentonville Road, London N1 9LG
Telephone: 0845 127 0060
Email: legacy@sense.org.uk
www.sense.org.uk

Registered Charity No. 289868
Patron: Her Royal Highness
The Princess Royal

sense
for deafblind people

Deafblindness – A Pioneering Approach

"Over 90% of what we learn about the world comes through our eyes and ears"

Sense is the leading national charity that supports and campaigns for children and adults who are deafblind. We provide expert advice and information as well as specialist services to deafblind people, their families, carers and the professionals who work with them..

Over 90% of what we learn about the world comes through our eyes and ears, so deafblind people need expert education from early on if they're not to withdraw into their own worlds.

advertisement feature

 **FOCUS** Birmingham

Supporting people with visual impairments and other disabilities, together with their carers, to live fulfilling and independent lives by providing services that reflect their wants and needs.

For more than 150 years, Focus Birmingham has provided support, care and advice to individuals with both sight loss and, in many cases, those with multiple disabilities. Through day and residential services, community services and hospital advise centres, each week more than 3000 people receive our support.

Our aim is to provide more services, to a wider group of people, over the coming years. But to enable us to do this we need additional support. Your legacy or bequest could mean:

- Additional community workers, offering advice on benefits, events and support services
- A new day service in different areas of the community
- Specialist mobile transport for those who use wheelchairs
- Further outreach activities, including supporting those with multiple disabilities in daily life (shopping, meals out, family outings)
- Increased awareness and development training
- Opportunities for engagement with social enterprise and learning schemes

FOCUS
Birmingham

Landing on the moon, seeing the Berlin Wall fall, following a star falling from the sky…

Watching grandchildren grow, reading a newspaper, telling a story…

Throughout our lives we all take these things for granted – whether it's a worldwide event or something more personal, we all assume that our eyesight and our ability to communicate will stay the same. But not everyone is that lucky.

For more than 150 years, Focus Birmingham has provided support, care and advice to individuals with both sight loss and, in many cases, those with multiple disabilities. Through day and residential services, community activities, helplines and advisers, training and hospital advice centres, each week more than 3000 people receive our support. At Focus each and every day is about enabling everyone to enjoy life and, in particular, to have fun!

We are extremely proud of our day centre, which provides specialist support and development opportunities, and that was only achieved by a legacy left to us by a local lady. The centre caters each day for over 50 members, ranging in age from 22 to 70, to undertake classes, learn music and IT skills, develop communication methods, attend riding and swimming lessons; it also provides access to physiotherapy, personal care and community outreach programmes.

During the last year, a small bequest left to us by a former service user has enabled us to purchase a specially adapted vehicle, which allows young people with mobility, communication and personal care needs, who often spend the majority of their day in wheelchairs, to participate in theatre visits and holidays. The vehicle serves 6 individuals at any one time, and requires a driver and a support worker. This is a step forward – but every day 50 others that contact us are unable to participate, because 1 vehicle is not enough.

A service user recently told us "without Focus' services, I would not be able to see the world around me. I don't mean that literally, as I have no sight, but Focus has found ways to help me understand many things, including colour, light and texture; all things I never imagined possible. I hope one day I can give something back." Focus views every person as a unique individual; not only do disabilities vary, so do abilities, desire and need. Each person we work with has a specialist package of support. In the majority of cases, this requires 1 member of staff to 1 individual. As you can imagine, this has a high price tag, but we know that everyone is worth it.

A vital service, unique to us, is the Low Vision Centre. Here, as well as providing advice on sight loss prevention, the centre staff undertake eye examinations, dispensing and diabetic retinopathy screening. The centre provides free lifetime loans of equipment such as magnifiers, and offers a counselling service to those recently affected by sight loss or disability.

Our aim is to provide more services, to a wider group of people, over the coming years. But to enable us to do this we need additional support. Your legacy or bequest could mean

- Additional community workers, offering advice on benefits, events and support services
- A new day service in different areas of the community
- Specialist mobile transport for those who use wheelchairs
- Further outreach activities, including supporting those with multiple disabilities in daily life (shopping, meals out, family outings)
- Increased awareness and development training
- Opportunities for engagement with social enterprise and learning schemes

When you have finished reading this, perhaps consider those who are unable to do so – and consider leaving Focus Birmingham a legacy, so we can make sure everyone gets the most out of their lives, whatever it takes.

Focus Birmingham – Supporting people with visual impairments and other disabilities, together with their carers, to live fulfilling and independent lives by providing services that reflect their wants and needs.

www.focusbirmingham.org.uk

maggie's
cancer caring centres

With Maggie's she doesn't have to face cancer alone

Few things are as devastating as cancer. It can leave you feeling isolated and full of despair. Maggie's is a unique haven of support, care and understanding for people coping with cancer, and their families. With a warm welcome, a cup of tea and specialist support services, we help take much of the fear and anxiety away and help people live with, through and beyond cancer.

We rely entirely on donations to do this. By remembering Maggie's in your Will – with any amount, large or small – you can help us give many more people facing cancer the love and support they need.
To find out more about leaving a legacy to Maggie's Cancer Caring Centres please call **0141 341 5674** or email **Ellen.Martin@maggiescentres.org** *Thank you.*

With your legacy we can be there

There's no place like Maggie's

Cancer touches so many lives, bringing with it fear, distress and confusion. Maggie's exists to turn cancer patients back into people and give them the special care and support they need. We're here for their family and friends too.

Our inspiring buildings and experienced cancer support specialists provide a warm welcome and help put people at ease. At Maggie's we believe that everyone's experience of cancer is different and that the support we offer must give them what they truly need. Sometimes that's simply a cup of tea, a chat with someone who understands and a space where they can be themselves. Or it may be practical help and advice, counselling or a course in relaxation. Whatever is needed, Maggie's provides a whole range of essential services to positively transform the way people live with cancer.

Right now there are six Maggie's Cancer Caring Centres, with six more under way. Our aim is to have a Maggie's alongside every major cancer treatment centre in the UK. However, our work is completely dependent on the generosity of people who believe in what we do and want to help us make a difference.

We understand that looking after your loved ones comes first. But when you've taken care of those who matter most, please consider remembering Maggie's in your Will. Whether your gift is large or small, it will help us keep our doors open for people dealing with the devastating impact of cancer for a long time to come.

To find out more about leaving a legacy to Maggie's Cancer Caring Centres please call 0141 341 5674 or email Ellen.Martin@maggiescentres.org .

Introduction

Everyone at some time or another finds themselves faced with making arrangements following the death of a loved one, whether a relative or close friend. At this distressing time, any mention of a will (much less the proving of it), or what assets the deceased owned, will be seen as an intrusion into personal grief, indeed an invasion of privacy at a time when you feel least able to cope.

This book cannot help in alleviating the suffering that will be felt with the loss of a loved one – dealing with grief is a very individual matter. What it can do is to provide information about what will be needed and what matters have to be dealt with in as straightforward and uncomplicated a manner as the subject allows. It tells you what to do and why, and how to go about it. It takes a step-by-step view of the necessary procedures from writing a will to estate planning and proving a will.

The first part of the book will be concerned with how to write a will. Basically you 'make' a will because you want to direct who receives your assets following your death. Occasionally, you may even want to ensure that certain people do not receive a share in your estate. You may have already made your will either with the help of a solicitor or on a standard proprietary will form available from most large newsagents. However, if you have not done either, then it is a matter that must be considered as an urgent task. If you have already made out a will, as your personal situations change it may become necessary to write a new will.

It is recommended that a new will be drawn up every five years, or less if there are any major changes in your life, such as marriage, inheritance, death or divorce. Any of these events should necessitate a revised will.

Examples of a basic will and specific clauses which may be added in different circumstances are also to be found. How to make an addition to your will (a *codicil*) is also shown.

Approximately one in every five persons writes their own will. In London the number is higher, one in every three, while in Scotland the figure is approximately one in every four. However, most people still go to a solicitor, not because their affairs are complex but because they do not know where to start or find the task daunting.

Estate planning and inheritance tax are examined in Chapter 6. For the inexperienced and unsure this subject can be not only bewildering but frightening too. You may feel more confident arranging for a consultation with a solicitor or tax consultant before planning your will. House prices in 2008 and so far in 2009 have shown a decrease of circa 17.9 per cent. This puts house values back to 2005. However, despite spousal/civil partner transfers on death, the threshold itself has not kept pace with the rising personal wealth over the last decade. It comes as no surprise that IHT has become seen as another stealth tax. Five per cent of all estates (32,000) pay this tax and it is expected that by 2015 there will be 4 million estates attracting IHT. Income from IHT in the tax year 2005/06 was estimated to generate £3.3 billion, 16 per cent higher than the £2.9 billion from the previous year, and has continued its increase in 2007/08. The majority, 90 per cent of all estates that pay IHT, are below £1 million. Halifax Group Economist Tim Crawford pointed out in his assessment in 2007 that an increasing number of people 'on modest incomes are now potentially liable' to this tax, which used to be considered to affect only the well-off. Therefore, more and more families find themselves, and will continue to find themselves, paying what used to be known as 'death' tax.

In Appendix 4 the local offices of the Probate Registry in England and Wales are listed. These offices are the first place to start. Appendix 4 also lists useful addresses for Scotland. Scottish law differs in many ways from the law of England and Wales. These differences are noted separately in Chapter 11.

Within the limitations of this book, the basic differences for both making and proving a will (and for obtaining confirmation in Scotland) are defined and clarified. However, should any complication arise then do seek professional advice. Indeed, in Scotland, professional advice at the commencement is recommended.

Naturally, if your affairs are complicated, with, perhaps, the existence of a trust fund, an existing business or other external factors which affect the estate, for example overseas property, then the best person to go to would be a solicitor. If the will is likely to be contested, a solicitor and possibly counsel will have to be used. If prior planning has not been done then a Deed of Family Arrangement varying the will of the deceased can be considered (see pages 106–08 for details) assuming the time frame for this allows action. Solicitors are experts not only in drawing up wills but on trust funds too, and can act as executors of an estate. You may feel that your estate would benefit from tax planning and therefore it is important to go and see your tax adviser. They may suggest making a Potentially Exempt Transfer (PET) whereby you gift certain investments or belongings to, say, your grandchildren via a trust. Your tax adviser would then discuss the drawing up of this document with your solicitor including how changes in the Trust tax law may affect your plans. However, do be aware that these services have to be paid for.

With recent Inheritance Tax changes, your original tax planning may need amendment. A solicitor's fee for dealing with an application for probate was previously based on the value of the estate (and some practices still use this as a guide) but now it refers to the length of time (and expenses known as dispersements) taken to handle your affairs. This will be based on an hourly charge of about £180 per hour (although there are some solicitors who charge more) plus expenses and VAT. This includes an administration cost in the form of a charge for letters received and letters sent, and the solicitor is supposed to notify you in writing of his/her charges with regard to this when he or she takes instructions. In the absence of such notification then do ask for a fee structure.

Payment provision for professionals handling probate matters needs to be made in your will as it is extremely unlikely that work will be done for free. However, elderly readers should beware of solicitors who include or suggest in any way whatsoever a bequest made to them. Law Society rules contained in the *Guide to the Professional Conduct of Solicitors*, eighth edition, make it clear what is acceptable and what is not. If you feel you are being pressured, then change your solicitor, write a codicil removing him/her as an executor and deleting any bequest and, finally, if you feel up to it, report the firm to Law Society Consumer Complaints (see address below).

As a co-executor and/or beneficiary, should you feel a solicitor's charge is too high or the work carried out is unsatisfactory, you should first put your complaint in writing to the firm. If it is not resolved to your satisfaction, then you can contact the Law Society in writing, explaining the circumstances and asking for its opinion. (Law Society Consumer Complaints, Victoria Court, 8 Dormer Place, Leamington Spa, Warwickshire CV32 5AE.) It is worth noting that presently the Law Society is one of the few professional bodies which actively adjudicates for fairness between the public and its members, but it does take persistence and time on your part. Whether or not the Law Society can effectively 'ride two horses' at the same time is open to debate.

Banks will also advise on preparing wills and dealing with probate matters. The fee route is similar to that of solicitors; however, in most instances, banks are more expensive.

Tax planning for your estate does not mean that the action taken by you or your advisers will ensure total safety from IHT. Chancellors have been known to change tax rules and recently, for the first time, backdate them in order to claim more tax back. Vigilance is therefore essential. Your advisers should keep you informed of any changes likely to affect you.

Once a will has been made it is no use placing it in an obscure unsafe location. You should inform your executor(s) where it will be kept. Indeed, it may be prudent to leave a copy of it with your solicitor or at your bank or with the Probate Registry which charges a one-off fee of £15.

If you die without leaving a will then the laws of intestacy apply to your estate. This means that your estate is divided between your lawful spouse and your surviving blood relatives according to specific rules laid down by Parliament. If there are no living relatives, once an extensive search has been undertaken, your money goes to the Crown.

These intestacy rules are, of course, made in broad terms and cannot take account of your individual wishes. So it is possible that a close relative whom you may not have wanted to be a beneficiary will take a share of your estate. Conversely, a close friend or relative by marriage whom you may wish to benefit will not do so unless you make a will.

In December 1993 the White Paper's recommendations regarding the financial position of the surviving spouse under intestacy rules were finally passed. Civil partners as well as spouses are included in the changes. From 1 February 2009, these changes have increased the surviving spouse's statutory legacy from £125,000 to £250,000 if there are children. If there are no children it increases from £200,000 to £450,000 (of course the estate has to have that value in it), and a life interest in half of the balance.

In October 1995 the government passed a new measure called the Law Reform (Succession) Act 1995 which came into effect on 1 January 1996. It amended the 1975 Inheritance Act. This amendment means that the vast majority of couples living outside wedlock can now seek financial provision from the estate of the deceased cohabitee, while at the same time it leaves open the claims from a separated wife and dependent children from any previous marriage.

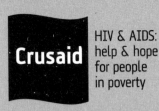

Crusaid

HIV & AIDS:
help & hope
for people
in poverty

A legacy of hope

Legacies made to Crusaid are transforming people's lives in the UK and across the world. The charity raises funds all year round for the 33 million people living with HIV and AIDS, but it's the legacies that Crusaid receives that make all the difference to its work.

Despite vital developments in medical care, HIV remains one of the fastest-growing killers in the world today with 2.7 million new diagnoses and 2 million deaths in the last year. The virus can leave people unable to work or care for themselves and, due to the social stigma attached to HIV and AIDS, isolated from help from the community.

Crusaid funds programmes in the UK and internationally to offer help and hope to people living in poverty as a result of HIV and AIDS. It has made over 45,000 grants in the UK through the Crusaid Hardship Fund, which has paid for necessities such as food, heating and a method of storing medication. Its international focus currently rests on Point of Light projects in Sub-Saharan Africa, which provide a safe place for vulnerable people to receive counselling, a hot meal, home-based care and welfare support.

Crusaid is 100 per cent reliant on donations to finance its crucial programmes and works hard to raise funds through activities such as the Crusaid Walk for Life, Europe's largest walk for HIV and AIDS. However, revenues from this type of fundraising are unpredictable and often restricted to specific programmes.

Legacy donations, however, help Crusaid to plan accurately for projects with a secure vision for the future. In return, Crusaid applies a rigorous system to ensure that legacy donations are directed where they are needed most: saving lives.

Just seven per cent of people leave money to charities in their wills, but it is this type of donation that allows Crusaid to fund special projects and expand its vital work.

To find out more about Crusaid and how to include the charity in your will, visit www.crusaid.org.uk or contact Jordan Hay, Head of Fundraising, Marketing & Communications on 020 7539 3897 or email jordanh@crusaid.org.uk

Reg charity no. 1011718

However, it must be stressed that the Act doesn't automatically give a common-law partner inheritance tax rights on intestacy, merely it seeks to *clarify* the standing of such partners in respect of claims made under the Inheritance (Provision for Family and Dependants) Act 1975. Section 1 of the 1995 Act rules that on intestacy or partial intestacy, a spouse will benefit in the estate provided he or she survives for 28 days after the date of death of the deceased. A spouse who survives for a short time but dies within the 28-day period will be treated as if he or she had died within the lifetime of the deceased.

The second part of the book deals with probate, what steps should be taken and when, in order to prove a will.

If the sad task of winding up the estate of a close relative or friend is placed under your agreed control, you may need to seek advice. The best place to start is at the Personal Applications Department of your nearest Probate Registry or at one of its sub-registries. The new call centre on 0845 3020900 can be used for IHT queries and for forms, and also a website at www.courtservice.gov.uk. The Registrar and his colleagues in the Personal Applications Department in your area deal on a daily basis with all sorts of queries raised regarding probate. However, they cannot give legal advice. Of course, the State has laid down certain rules which have to be followed by them. The rules are there to protect the wishes of the deceased and to ensure that those wishes are fulfilled.

Wills can be rejected because they are invalid but most are accepted as having been properly made according to the laws applicable. The Registrar has some discretion in respect of what may be accepted without query but also has rules to follow. He or she cannot, of course, change a will nor give an opinion as to its meaning other than for the specific purpose of deciding who may be entitled to be appointed to administer the estate. If the will is being challenged with valid reason and proof, for example lack of testamentary capacity, then the Probate Registrar will refer you on to the High Court Family section or possibly the Chancery Court in order for the validity of the will to be heard before a judge.

If your affairs are complicated or involved, this book is not for you. Unless you have the right legal training (or knowledge) you may have to call upon your professional legal adviser in at least one aspect. But the fact that your estate is of considerable value does not in itself create problems except, of course, in inheritance tax planning. The legal procedure to follow is the same whether an estate has little value or great value.

If tax planning is needed, then do seek assistance from a tax consultant. Up until recently, trusts were the mainstay of tax planning but with the changes implemented in 2006 and updates in 2007, 2008, and now 2009, care is needed when deciding on this route. Trusts cost money to start and administer.

In probably 95 per cent of cases a layperson is capable of dealing with his or her own affairs without any assistance from professionals. For this majority who feel capable and confident and able to cope within constraints this book is here as a guide.

Finally, it is possible to revise the terms of a deceased's will through a document called a Deed of Family Arrangement provided all the beneficiaries of that will agree to the change(s) and are over 18 years of age. It also has to be done within two years from the date of death. Importantly, HM Revenue & Customs has to agree these changes and be notified of them within six months of the death. The will itself is not actually altered but the estate is divided up in the agreed manner and its effect is recognised by HMRC for IHT purposes.

Remember the
humble donkeys
in your Will,
and we will remember you...

In the UK, Ireland and other parts of Europe, we provide permanent refuge to neglected and unwanted donkeys and have taken over 13,000 into our care since we started in 1969.

To find out how your contribution can help prevent the suffering of donkeys and how you will be remembered for your kindness, please contact our Founder:

Dr Elisabeth Svendsen, MBE,
The Donkey Sanctuary
Dept HWW, Sidmouth,
Devon, EX10 0NU
Tel. 01395 578222 Fax. 01395 579266
Email. enquiries@thedonkeysanctuary.com
Website. www.thedonkeysanctuary.org.uk

FRSB

give with confidence

The **Donkey** Sanctuary

WORKING WORLDWIDE

1

Why Do You Need a Will?

For most people the thought of making a will is depressing, confirming the inevitability of our fate, and because of this it is often put aside for another day. Granted, such a gloomy task is hardly inspiring. However, sooner or later the task has to be done as it is an essential part of administering your personal affairs and taking responsibility.

Most people own their own car and have household furniture, bank and/or building society accounts, and a growing number own a house, and some a second home from either inheritance or purchase – and add to that the ownership of shares. By making a will you are directing who should receive your possessions following your death – it is effectively your last statement of your intentions. Without a will you are considered to have died *intestate* and the intestacy laws apply. In Scottish and English law if there are no traceable surviving relatives then all of your possessions, in other words 'your estate', less any debts or liabilities, go to the Crown.

The greater percentage of the population at present do not bother to make a will. How many times have you said: 'I do not have that much to leave, so why bother to make out a will?' Or, 'Why should it concern me who will get what? I will, after all, not be around.' Or, lastly, 'Estate planning? I won't have to pay the tax.'

Emma arrived at Barnardo's so traumatised by abuse that she couldn't speak and was very frightened of adults. So it was a special moment when, after 14 months of patient nurturing, Emma reached out to take her foster mum's hand for the first time.

Vulnerable children like Emma need someone to care for and believe in them and that's exactly what Barnardo's does. We work directly with over 100,000 children, young people and their families every year. We run vital projects across the UK, including counselling for children who have been abused as well as fostering and adoption services.

We do this because we believe all children deserve the best start in life, no matter what they have been through. And to us it's so rewarding when a little girl like Emma begins to reach out and trust again.

advertisement feature

We know Emma still has a long way to go.

And so does Barnardo's, especially if we are to secure our work in the future.

To carry out our work, we rely on the donations that people so kindly remember to include in their Wills. Currently these gifts make up almost half of all the money given to us by the public. These donations are our lifeblood and every generous gift in Will, no matter how large or small, helps to sustain our vital work.

We understand that family and loved ones come first. But you can help us continue supporting children like Emma for as long as we are needed by including a gift to Barnardo's alongside the people and causes that are dear to you.

And because we know what a precious gift a legacy is, Barnardo's makes a special promise to supporters who remember us in this way.

You would expect us to make the best use of your gift for the benefit of vulnerable children. You would also expect us to treat you and your family with courtesy, sensitivity and respect.

We promise to do this and to provide you with the information and confidential advice you need to make your decision. We promise too that we will not press you to tell us what decision you have made. If we ask about your gift it is so that we can say thank you, and we understand if you prefer not to tell us.

If you would like more information about Barnardo's work or would like to see a copy of our promise to supporters, please contact giftsinwills@barnardos.org.uk or call 020 8498 7880.

Thank you.

Please help us to pass on the message about how important donations in Wills are to our work

In the UK, ONE IN FOUR people will die from Cancer

Help stop cancer before it starts

World Cancer Research Fund (WCRF UK)
19 Harley Street, London W1G 9QJ
Tel: 020 7343 4205 Email: legacy@wcrf.org
Registered with the Charity Commission in England and Wales (Registered Charity No: 1000739)

World Cancer
Research Fund

World Cancer Research Fund is the principal UK charity dedicated to the prevention of cancer through the promotion of healthy diet and nutrition, physical activity and weight management. It is committed to providing cancer research and education programmes, which educate people about choices they can make to reduce their chances of developing cancer. By spreading the good news that cancer can be prevented, World Cancer Research Fund hopes that many thousands of lives will be saved.

World Cancer Research Fund receives no government funding for its scientific research programmes, so this vital work is only made possible through the generosity of individual donations, with legacies being a very important means of support. Leaving a gift in your will to us would help ensure less people are affected by this terrible disease and what better legacy to leave to your loved ones – a future free from cancer.

Your legacy could help stop cancer before it starts.

World Cancer
Research Fund

The wealth of this nation has dramatically increased over the past 15 years despite the current credit crunch. It is not just the privileged few who have money and assets to leave to their family and friends. The increase in house prices was one of the most significant adjustments to personal wealth in the early to mid 2000s. In addition, increasing numbers of the second generation are inheriting a property or indeed have purchased a second home. And a few may own yet another property in this country or overseas, which may be rented out. Indeed, a study by merchant bankers Morgan Grenfell showed that the annual number of inherited properties rose in the last decade by one-third to 128,000. The value of inherited property quadrupled to £8.5 billion with the long-term forecast showing that this will rise even further in the next two decades as 21 million people (86 per cent of them will be pensioners) will be homeowners. The predicted windfalls are estimated to total £35 billion a year!

A survey conducted in spring 2005 by the Halifax gives the figure of 2.4 million houses valued above the threshold value of £275,000 (2005/06). The Halifax survey claims that over the past few years an increase of 160 per cent in the number of estates falling into IHT has arisen and it is estimated that a further 5 per cent will fall into this tax in addition to last year's figure. In order to maintain the IHT threshold into real terms with the increase in property prices, and not including any other assets, then the threshold would have to be in excess of £400,000, even with the recent downturn in property prices.

When you add the value of house prices to even modest savings, insurance policies and so on, you can easily see how the inheritance tax threshold of £325,000 means that more and more people are affected.

The 2006 Budget introduced sweeping tax changes on trusts. One of the major alterations to existing trusts (that is, those in existence at 22 March 2006) is that the age limit of absolute gift has altered from 25 to 18 years. For accumulation and maintenance trusts, for example, if an existing trust as at 22 March 2006 had not amended its agreement at the latest by 5 April 2008, to deliver its proceeds absolutely to the beneficiary or beneficiaries when they reach 18 years of age, then every 10 years from the commencement of the trust a charge of inheritance tax of 4.2 per cent will be levied under the 10-year rule. There has been a further 6-month extension to the April 2008 date. For trusts whose beneficiary or beneficiaries are disabled, there might be a certain relaxation of the rules.

The objection to this change is that 18-year-olds are not as mature as 25-year-olds, and if the money accumulated for someone's benefit is given to him or her at 18, this could lead to it being spent on, for example, a fast sports car rather than being kept for the educational purposes or a deposit for a home for which it was initially intended.

If you have a trust or intend to create a trust with your will, it is important that you seek professional advice.

Inheritance tax is generally regarded as a tax on middle England as the wealthy take great care to provide for continuity of wealth in future generations. The middle classes are more reluctant to prepare for this tax, considering the expense in their lifetime, with the end result that most of the contributions to this tax come from the middle classes, and it often affects the people who can least afford it.

For those of you undecided on estate planning, it is worth recalling Gordon Brown's words when he was Shadow Chancellor. When his predecessor announced in his Autumn Statement in 1995 that inheritance tax was due to be increased to £200,000 in the 1996/97 tax year, Mr Brown stated his disappointment at this action. Although the inheritance tax threshold has been increased to £325,000, the number of estates liable to this tax has also increased. Mr Brown and now Mr Darling, have the distinction of raising more tax than 'squeeze them till the pips squeak' Chancellor Healey in the late 1970s.

For those readers who are collectors of works of art, HM Revenue & Customs (HMRC) has produced a conditionally exempt works of art register. Conditional exemption from inheritance tax may be granted for works of art and other objects, such as pictures, prints, books, manuscripts and scientific collections which are of national, scientific, historic or artistic interest. The rules for this conditional exemption are that the owner must keep the object in the United Kingdom and allow reasonable public access to the object. Readers can gain further details by obtaining booklet IR67 entitled 'Capital Taxation and the National Heritage' from the Capital Taxes Offices.

A growing number of couples now choose to live together outside marriage. Many items, such as the house, are bought jointly. However, until the Law Reform (Succession) Act 1995, which came into effect on 1 January 1996, the surviving cohabitee did not as of right receive any portion of the deceased's estate *unless* provision had been made in the will. Under this new Bill, the surviving cohabitee does not have an automatic right of inheritance but can claim financial provision from the deceased's estate.

Further amendments with regard to the rights of same-sex partners and other cohabitees came into force in December 2005 through the Civil Partnership Act.

Problems can occur when writing your own will. The most frequent problem with DIY wills is that they are not worded clearly. State clearly and precisely your intentions. For example, in Scotland a will, apart from the signatures of the witnesses, must also include the witnesses' full details such as names, addresses and occupations. Again in Scotland, if the will is handwritten by the testator, ie a holograph will, witnesses are not required.

If there is a rule when writing your own will it must be to keep it simple. Do not stray into legal technicalities. Instead, set out in writing what gifts are to be made, clearly identifying all objects, stating who should receive them, and ensuring that you are gifting items that belong to you. You should include details such as full names and current addresses of your executors and any beneficiaries, and in the case of charities, their registration number.

A will does not come into effect until death has occurred. A testator does not become a testator until he or she dies, nor does an executor become an executor until this happens. So until this event the contents of a will and a will itself can be changed. If there are minor alterations, these changes can be inserted in the form of a codicil. If changes occur frequently or if they are major ones, it is better to write a new will. Remember, if a new will is drawn up, the old one must be destroyed, provided, of course, that you are satisfied that the new one has been drawn up properly and signed and witnessed correctly with the important statement at its beginning (see page 82, clause C), 'I hereby revoke all former wills, codicils and testamentary provisions at any time made by me and declare this to be my last will.'

You can also include in your will any specific arrangements you may wish to make regarding your own funeral. Or perhaps you may wish to donate your body to medical research or to donate your organs. Your wish with regard to organ donations needs to be known by those closest to you in order for them to fulfil your wishes. So a will is used not only for listing who should receive what asset from your estate but also for any other wishes you may have to make, for example, funeral arrangements and donation of organs. Your executor should also be made aware of certain provisions in your will, namely organ donation because time is of the essence.

Since 1964, even if you hold a foreign passport but are still permanently resident in this country, there is no distinction in law between owning property in the United Kingdom (under English law) and leaving it in your will to a person who resides abroad. Property can also be held overseas and left to someone residing in this country.

Distribution of immoveable property held overseas has to be carried out in accordance with the law of the land in which that property is situated. In some cases, the will must be made in a specific way to dispose of the property, eg Spain insists on a will made before a notary. This should serve as a reminder, when purchasing property overseas, to enquire what inheritance tax laws apply there. Legal advice in such cases should always be sought. See a brief section on page 58.

Who can make a will?

1. A child under the age of 18 cannot generally make a will.

Help us continue the fight against
Glaucoma

Making a Will is not just essential for the sake of your loved ones it is also a wonderful opportunity to make the world a better place.

Glaucoma is the leading cause of preventable blindness in the UK. By leaving a gift to our charity in your Will, you can help us give the support and information people need to stop this insidious condition from stealing their sight; and fund essential clinical research that would free future generations from glaucoma.

For more information on how to leave a gift in your Will to the IGA, please contact our Legacy Officer on 01233 64 81 64

Thank you for such a precious gift.

INTERNATIONAL GLAUCOMA ASSOCIATION
Woodcote House, 15 Highpoint Business Village,
Henwood,Ashford, Kent TN24 8DH
Sightline 01233 64 81 70
Administration 01233 64 81 64
Email info@iga.org.uk
Website: www.glaucoma-association.com

International Glaucoma Association **iga**

The Charity for People with Glaucoma

Charity registered in England & Wales No. 274681

However, if you are under the age of 18 and in Her Majesty's armed forces on active service, then you will be able to make a will which will stand as a valid one.

2. A person of sound mind.
Obviously a person must be of sound mind and capable of managing his or her affairs when signing a will, in other words they must have 'testamentary capacity'. However, if after making your will you become unsound of mind through illness or an accident, the will remains valid. If you make a will after you have become diagnosed as mentally incapable, then your will can be challenged and ruled invalid and, if the diagnosis is upheld, then an earlier will is usually reinstated, or intestacy rules applied. Under Section 96 1E of the Mental Health Act, if a judge is present then he or she is empowered to make a will on behalf of an incapable person.

The Mental Health Act defines a person suffering from severe subnormality as one who is in a state 'of incomplete development of mind which includes sub-normality of intelligence and is of such a nature or degree that the patient is incapable of living an independent life or of guarding himself against serious exploitation or will be so incapable of an age to do so'. Lord Chief Justice Templeman set out a guide for solicitors to use when faced with the potential scenario of incapacity. He advises to have a doctor present who specialises in old age medicine in order to confirm the capacity of the person.

Great Uncle Herbert talking to himself in the garden or your grandmother losing objects is not necessarily cause for challenging either will in court. In all probability they would not be seen as being of unsound mind but possibly suffering from a mild dose of eccentricity. On the other hand, if a person is so disorientated that they are uncertain where they are when in their own home and are unable to look after themselves may be grounds to bring this Act into force. Sudden and dramatic changes in prior line of inheritance to favour one sibling totally against another could mean that undue influence or possibly more devious practices have occurred. Expert legal and medical opinions are essential in this instance but do not rely on the courts to meter out justice, as this does not happen in all cases.

Decide on your aims

Before making a will think what you want to achieve by it. Are you married? Have you any children? Are there any other beneficiaries you wish to include, such as parents, brothers, sisters, distant relatives? Are you likely to leave any money to charity? Have you considered organ donation?

Once you have considered what you want to achieve then draw up a list noting exactly what assets you have, the approximate value, and how best to distribute your estate to fulfil your wishes. If you have children under 18 then you have to consider and act by selecting suitable people as guardians, and perhaps trustees. Any assets left to minors are held in a trust until 18 years of age or until the age specified in your will.

Whatever you own is considered to be an *asset*: a car, any items of furniture, jewellery, paintings, house, securities and so on. Add to this any money you may have in savings accounts, along with details of any insurance policies or investments you hold. Literally, everything of value you own should be listed, from half shares in the family silver to half shares in an old jalopy.

Now list, in order of priority, those people you wish to benefit from your will. You may want your daughter to have all your jewellery and a friend might appreciate a specific item such as a ring, a painting or any item that holds particular fond memories. If you are a parent or have a partner, you will probably wish them to receive the money from your life insurance policy, a share of the house, any pension rights you have, investments and so on. You might want your church or favourite charities to receive a sum of money. Whatever you decide, note alongside each item whom you wish it to go to.

A will is the 'last wish' of a person and so expresses what you want to happen after your death. However, some wishes may not be actionable. For example, if you do not ask the people who you have selected to be your executors whether they are prepared to take on the task, they could well turn it down, even if they had previously agreed to undertake this role. You may wish to be buried in your local churchyard, but without prior permission from the vicar you may be put to rest in another cemetery. And if you died while living abroad but wished to be buried in this country, arrangements would have to be made (and finance found) to bring your body back.

Again, another example is that of guardianship, briefly mentioned previously. If you wish to appoint a person or persons as your children's guardians in the case of your and your spouse's death, then do ensure that you have their agreement and that they are willing to take on this responsibility should you die young. Importantly, consider carefully if they hold the love and respect of your children and vice versa. Also, you will need to have a special guardianship document drawn up by your solicitor to ensure this happens – see page 38.

How much will my estate be worth in, say, 20 years' time?

How long is a piece of string? This eventuality is, however, taken care of. Your executor values your estate at the date of death.

Any items not specially mentioned in your will would come under the term 'residue of estate', in other words everything you own or have legal title to and which has not been already left under your will. Whoever is left the residue of the estate would inherit the additional items not already disposed of. But, to ensure that a newly acquired specific gift goes to the right person, as your personal circumstances change so should your will. Every few years examine your present situation and, if necessary, make out a new will. If there are only minor amendments to be made, then a codicil can be drawn up.

Civil Partnership Bill

In December 2005 same-sex civil partners were for the first time able to commit to each other when the Civil Partnership Bill came into force.

Same-sex couples now receive tax breaks previously unavailable to them. The most important of these is the transfer of assets from one to another without incurring CGT or IHT liabilities. The downside is, should the cohabiting couple in a civil partnership own two properties, then like a married couple, they can only claim one allowance on one property between them. For income tax, there remains no benefit for married couple's allowance (MCA) if neither of the civil partners have a birth date after 6 April 1935 as the Chancellor, Gordon Brown, withdrew the married couple's allowance when he first came into office.

For couples, married or in civil partnerships, where one person has a greater disposable income and is thinking of putting money into a trust for the other person, the money will be taxed as if it still belongs to the more affluent partner. For cohabiting couples without this civil partnership, it is taxable on the recipient's income.

Civil partners, as well as married partners, can transfer their deceased partner's national insurance contributions into their own name, thus enhancing their pension when they reach pensionable age.

There were many needs for this Act to come into place, not least of which was for same-sex couples who wished to commit to each other to be able to do so. Civil partners in intestacy now have the same statutory rights on the deceased partner's estate as married couples.

Under English law there is no such thing as a common-law husband or wife. Should a couple break up and not have a *cohabitation contract* then there is no legal provision for maintenance payments, for example, irrespective of how long the couple have cohabited. If property has not been purchased as tenants-in-common and there is no note in a legal document setting out precise percentage ownership, then proof of financial contributions has to be shown. However, this Act has not dampened disquiet about the lack of legislative protection for cohabiting couples who do not wish to formalise their relationship, and Ministers are examining ways of a later inclusion in this Act to enhance protection for these people. This is likely to take some time, however.

THEY DEPEND ON EACH OTHER, BUT THEIR FUTURE IS UP TO PEOPLE LIKE YOU.

Poor families depend upon their horses and donkeys to earn a living. If anything happens to that animal, they'll probably starve. **PLEASE REMEMBER SPANA IN YOUR WILL.**

We provide veterinary care for the working animals on which so many people around the world depend for a living. **SPANA has been helping working animals in North Africa and the Middle East for over eighty years.** But the owners are just as grateful for the work we do. Without us, many animals would suffer because their owners simply cannot afford the veterinary care they need. Your gift will ensure that our vital welfare work will continue, helping both working animals and the people who depend on them for an income, both now and in the future.

Please help sick and injured animals, and the people whose lives depend on them by remembering SPANA in your Will.

To find out more about **SPANA**, visit: **www.spana.org**.

For more information about how to remember us in your will and receive a free copy of our Will writing guide, call us on: **0207 831 3999** or write to:

SPANA, DEPT HTW10, FREEPOST LON20570, LONDON WC1N 2BR.

SPANA
Caring for Working Animals
WORLDWIDE

SPANA, 14 John Street, London WC1N 2EB Tel: 020 7831 3999 Fax: 020 7831 5999 Email: legacies@spana.org Registered Charity No. 209015. Registered in England. Company No. 558085

2

What Happens if You Die without a Valid Will?

If you die without leaving a valid will, you are said to have died *intestate*. Usually in instances where one spouse dies before the other, depending on the estate's size, all or the greatest share of the estate goes to the surviving spouse.

The present intestacy laws date back to 1858 when Probate Registries were first introduced. Since then they have been regularly updated to try to take account of the changes in personal circumstances and the change in the value of money.

The intestacy law, however, was considered by some to need a complete review. The general opinion was that this law no longer adequately met the needs for distributing the average person's estate and has subsequently been altered. Now if there is a surviving spouse and issue, then the spouse receives a lump sum, known as the *statutory legacy*, and half of the remaining estate for his or her life. *Life interest* means that the spouse cannot spend the capital of the life interest and may only use the interest obtained from investing that sum. The statutory legacy has been increased to £250,000 if the deceased leaves issue. The value increases to £450,000 if there are no children, provided that the estate has that amount of value in it, plus a life interest in half of the balance if there are parents, siblings or surviving nieces and nephews.

Present rules

As the intestacy law stands, if a person without a spouse dies with no will in place and leaves a child or other issue, then such person(s) will benefit from the realisation of all investments, property, etc on reaching the age of 18. If he or she is not 18, then the share is held in trust until the child reaches the age of majority, when usually he or she is able to receive it. However, the trustees may, in certain circumstances, advance monies from the trust for the purpose of 'maintenance, education or advancement of the child'. When the child attains 18 years and eventually receives the trust's estate it should include any interest earned on the money, assuming no payments of interest have been made to him or her.

It cannot be stressed too often that the prime importance of making a will is that you are able to specify whom you wish to deal with your affairs and to whom you wish to leave your estate. If you do not make a will and you die leaving no traceable relatives, your estate will go to the Crown and will form part of government funds. By making a will and appointing an executor(s), one of the advantages is the flexibility allowed to that executor(s) to move money around in a variable market in order to make the safest investment for your appointed heirs, although there are restrictions as to the nature of such investments.

If an executor has not been appointed in a will or a named executor refuses to act, or if a will has not been made out, then the deceased's property, including personal belongings, will be administered by a personal representative. This representative is appointed by the Probate Registry in accordance with strict rules of priority. These rules state that where there is no will, a spouse has the first right to be appointed to administer the deceased's estate. If there is a will the residuary beneficiary will have priority. But if the surviving spouse does not feel willing or able to handle the job, the couple's children may be appointed to act on their parent's behalf. When there is no surviving spouse or children then the task of administering the estate can fall on close relatives, ie parents, brothers, sisters or their issue. A close friend may be appointed attorney by the person entitled to act and, if suitable, will be appointed administrator, although this does not often happen.

Whoever is appointed has a duty to administer the estate to see that, where necessary, the assets are sold at the best possible price and any debts and expenses paid off. Once that has been done, distribution takes place in accordance with the Administration of Estates Act. This Act governs the distribution of an estate when the deceased has died intestate. Under the Act, if you were the appointed representative, you would have the power to deal with the estate as you thought fit in order to safeguard the assets. Of course, you are accountable for your actions.

You can claim administrative costs and out-of-pocket expenses from the estate, such as stamps, telephone calls and so on. Also, if you have had to forfeit a day's pay in attending to estate affairs you can reclaim the amount of pay lost, but you cannot charge for your time.

After *letters of administration* have been granted by the Probate Registry and once all debts and expenses have been paid, distribution can take place. Again, there is an order of priority.

If there is a surviving spouse *and* issue, the spouse receives all the deceased's personal items (known as *personal effects*) together with a sum up to the value of the statutory legacy, which is £250,000. Should the value of the estate exceed this and there is also issue, then the surviving spouse would receive life interest in half of the balance of the estate for life – in other words, the half of what remains after the personal effects, the statutory legacy of £250,000, and debts and expenses have been deducted. The remaining half would go to any children immediately, except if they are under the age of 18. If any child did die in the lifetime of the deceased leaving children of his or her own, then those children would divide their parent's share between them.

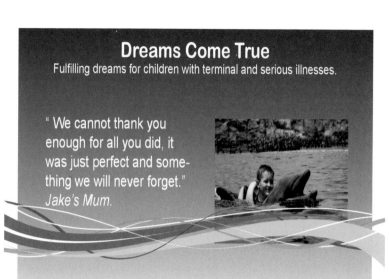

On the death of the surviving spouse the half of the estate which he or she has had a life interest in would pass to the children. Therefore, it is important to understand fully what *life interest* means. Life interest could be described as borrowed ownership in that you have the right to use the interest from the capital but cannot touch the capital as it does not legally belong to you. Upon death, the life interest passes to the other beneficiaries, for example the children, and is divided up equally for their benefit. Again, if any children of the deceased died in his or her lifetime leaving children of their own, then the same applies as in the previous paragraph. Do note, however, that some jointly owned assets may pass to the joint surviving owner irrespective of the intestacy rules.

When children are the nearest surviving relatives of the deceased, the estate passes to them and, if some have already died leaving children of their own, their share passes to their issue, ie grandchildren or great-grandchildren of the testator. The shares are held in a *statutory trust* for the children, in equal parts, until each reaches the age of 18 or marries, whichever happens first. The definition of children now includes legitimate, illegitimate or legally adopted children but not stepchildren.

In a case where there is a surviving spouse but *no* issue, the spouse's statutory legacy increases to £450,000 in addition to the personal effects. If the estate is larger than this and there are no surviving issue, but other relations are alive, such as parents, brothers, sisters, etc, then the spouse receives all the personal effects together with £450,000 and life interest in half of the residue of the estate absolutely.

If a brother or sister of the deceased dies in the deceased's lifetime, leaving children, then their children will take the deceased parent's share divided equally between them.

Should a person die leaving a surviving spouse but no children, or other issue, or indeed parents, brothers or sisters or their issue, the surviving spouse receives the whole of the estate, irrespective of its value.

The order of inheritance of an estate where the deceased has died intestate is as follows:

1. spouse;
2. children or, if they are deceased, their issue;
3. parents;
4. brothers and sisters of the 'whole blood' or, if deceased, their issue (such issue will divide their deceased parent's share between them);
5. brothers and sisters of the 'half blood' (having one common parent with the deceased) or, if deceased, their issue;
6. grandparents;
7. uncles and aunts of the 'whole blood' or, if deceased, their issue;
8. uncles and aunts of the 'half blood' or, if deceased, their issue;
9. and if there are none of the above, then the estate goes to the Crown.

Often you will see a notice in the national or local papers asking for the relatives of the deceased to contact a firm of solicitors. This usually means that the administrators are trying to trace relatives of the deceased. There is a time stipulation, however. A person cannot turn up some four years after the advertisement to claim his or her inheritance; by then it will be too late, though it is wise for an administrator to take out some form of indemnity cover if there are known beneficiaries who cannot as yet be traced.

Sadly, disputes do arise whether or not you leave a will. However, the existence of a will, provided it is properly worded, means that these disputes can be reduced. Legal advice should always be taken in these instances.

From 1 January 1996, common-law wives receive an income from the deceased partner's estate and property rights, provided they have lived together for two or more years. This right to benefit is not given under the succession laws but must be claimed by separate application to a court.

In cases of intestacy in England and Wales if a marriage has ended in divorce and a decree absolute has been granted, the divorced spouse is not entitled to any part of the estate. Their children being also children of the deceased, however, will be beneficiaries. If death took place after decree nisi had been given but before the granting of decree absolute, then a spouse would still be seen in the eyes of the law to be the surviving spouse and would benefit accordingly. A spouse does not benefit if a judicial separation decree has been issued. Such decrees are treated in the same manner as a divorce. A separation order issued by magistrates does not affect entitlement to benefit.

A divorce in England and Wales (for Scotland, see page 182) alters your previously made will and makes any gift to your ex-spouse void. However, the application of the law that creates this effect on other persons in your will may not operate as you would expect. It is very important, therefore, that a new will be made out when major events alter your life. Remember that once the new will has been written, signed and witnessed, you must destroy the old one.

When a person makes a will and then later marries, in England and Wales such a will is completely revoked or in some circumstances only revoked in part unless it states that it is being made 'in contemplation of' that forthcoming marriage to a named person, and, importantly, also states that the will is to remain in force after that marriage. If you are considering making a will before an anticipated marriage and you wish for the will to continue after your marriage, you would be strongly advised to consult a solicitor for advice.

3

What You Should Know before Writing a Will

Anything that is fully owned by you can be left in a will. Certain assets, such as those owned under a joint ownership which are already subject to an agreement to be passed on to the survivor, cannot be given. Also, any property which has been left to a person under a *form of nomination* (for instance, a National Savings Bank account) is not covered by your will even if it is referred to.

As years pass by, the value of most possessions usually increases. A will written 10 or 15 years ago may be outdated as, it is to be hoped, your possessions will have increased substantially in both quantity and value and your priorities may have changed. This is why it is important to update your will by making a new one. You may also be the beneficiary of someone else's will and may wish to name the person who, in turn, is to inherit this gift in your will. Incidentally, provided that you survive the donor, you, and ultimately your beneficiaries, will inherit the gift, assuming you have not disposed of it. You may be a partner in a business or a director, in which case the portion of your estate which refers to your business will be subject to your partnership agreement.

"Without The Prince's Trust I'd be stuck on a downward spiral."

You know what success feels like

Through hard work, determination and the right support, you've achieved great things.

Sadly, in each generation, there are young people who've never had anyone to point them in the right direction. For one reason or another they gave up on themselves and all they have to pass on to the next generation is a sense of hopelessness and failure.

Will you help us to break this cycle?

A legacy to The Prince's Trust will change young lives for the better and forever. By supporting our programmes, you'll bring hope to young people who just need a chance to succeed. The impact could last generations into the future.

With your support, we can give young people something very special – a future.

For more information about our work please email us at getinvolved@princes-trust.org.uk or call us on 020 7543 7316.

Prince's Trust

Prince's Trust

The Prince's Trust is the UK's leading youth charity helping change young lives

We give practical and financial support to 14-30 year olds, enabling them to develop skills that will help them move into education, employment or training.

Our priority is to help young people who are:

→ educational underachievers
→ offenders and ex-offenders
→ unemployed
→ in or leaving care

Our work is important because:

→ more than one million young people in the UK are not in work, education or training
→ the UK economy loses £10 million a day due to youth unemployment
→ youth crime costs the UK £1 billion each year

Since 1976 we have helped over 600,000 young people and we support 100 more each day.

To continue our work, we need to raise around £1 million every week.

For more information on The Prince's Trust please visit www.princes-trust.org.uk

This does not mean rewriting your will every year but assessing every few years whether your existing will still adequately covers all your wishes and, indeed, whether your personal circumstances have changed.

Guardianship

The appointment of guardians and their rights are governed by The Children Act 1989 amended by the Adoption and Children Act 2002. The child has to be under 18 years of age. As a parent, you have a parental responsibility to appoint a guardian by will (testamentary guardian) or by a document, the latter providing the appointment on your death. The appointed guardian's duties come into effect at the date of death providing there is no surviving parent with parental responsibility and a residence order in your sole favour relating to your son or daughter. Similar to appointing a testator, you should consult with the proposed guardian and get his or her agreement before including their name.

The unmarried parent of a child may acquire parental responsibility provided he or she registered this.

Should you, as a surviving parent, remarry or commit to a civil partnership, your new spouse/partner may acquire parental responsibility for a step-child by agreement or by court orders. This step-parent cannot appoint a guardian. On practical matters, clearly you should discuss this issue with the proposed guardian(s), gaining their agreement. This proposed guardian most certainly should respect and love your children and, importantly, know of your wishes.

You should consult with a solicitor who specialises in this subject. The Law Society website lists firms and notes the areas of the partners' expertise.

What is termed as 'property'?

Whatever you own from a house to personal effects is your *property*, and forms your *estate*.

In addition, there is a distinction between freehold and leasehold property not only in definition but, more importantly, in the context of this book, in the way it forms part of your estate. Owning the freehold of the land and buildings means it is yours for perpetuity. Leasehold property is only owned by you for the duration of the leasehold tenancy, for the remaining life of the lease. Leasehold property usually starts its life on a tenancy of 99 years or, in some unusual instances, 999 years. As time passes, so the lease's term decreases until the expiry date is reached.

So you can in theory leave your leasehold flat or house to your nearest relations. However, if the leasehold agreement states that you cannot assign the lease without consent of the owner of the lease, then your executor would first have to seek his or her permission before selling the property or assigning the lease to your beneficiaries. You can, of course, write to the lease owner and ask him to sell the lease of your house to you, but you only have the automatic legal right to purchase if you have lived there for four or more years. For owners of flats, luckily, legislation now gives the flat owner the right to purchase the lease of a flat. Consult your solicitor on this matter if you intend to exercise your right. Your lease may have under 30 years left and again you would need to seek advice should you wish this extended. Property with a short life of lease left shows a marked decrease in value.

Another direction that you can include in your will is with regard to the disposal of your body. You may wish to give particular directions for your funeral or even for what you want to have done with your body. Today it is becoming increasingly popular to carry donor cards which can be obtained at doctors' surgeries or from the National Transplant list based in Bristol. These cards authorise the use of various organs in your body for transplant purposes after your death in order to save or enhance lives. The organs are removed shortly after death once the donor card(s) has been passed on to the doctor or subject to your nearest of kin's agreement. The next of kin can also give authorisation for removal of organs once a patient has been pronounced dead. Do ensure that your next of kin is fully aware of your wish to save and promote life after yours has ended, and that he or she will fulfil this intention.

Financial matters

Insurance policies

There are three main types of insurance policy that will pay out on death. First there is a *life policy*, which, upon proof that death has occurred, ie a death certificate, will pay out the insured amount absolutely to a beneficiary named in the policy.

There is a further type of term insurance called the *family income benefit*. While a standard life insurance would pay out a fixed lump sum upon proof of death, family income benefit, acting as a replacement wage, would pay out each and every year throughout its term. There is an added benefit in that the amount can be made inflation proof.

This policy is not only applicable to men but should be considered by women as well. More and more women are wage earners but a fair proportion still remain at home looking after their children. For men, should a 'stay at home' mother die, how will the husband afford to hire a live-in nanny to care for their children? The cost of a nanny or home help varies but on average you would pay £10,000 to £20,000 and more a year, plus National Insurance contributions, depending on the individual's qualifications, experience, duties and hours of work and where you live.

This is another area that needs in-depth consideration. The stress that the death of a partner brings is bad enough without the added worry of insufficient money to cover the basic bills. The surviving spouse needs time to come to terms with his or her grief and that of their children rather than worrying where the next pound is coming from or having to work all hours to make ends meet. Thinking that parents will step in and help is not a practical alternative as in many cases this is not possible through ill-feelings, poor health or lack of money themselves.

The family income benefit's term is based on the youngest member of the family. So if you have three children ranging in age from 3 to 15, the policy would pay out for 15 years until the youngest child reached the age of 18.

If the policy's period of time is 12 years and you die six months into that term, your family will benefit. There is a minus side: if you die 11 years and six months into a 12-year policy, your family will only receive payment for the remaining portion of time, namely six months. You can hedge your bets, however, by taking out a *level-term policy*, which would pay out the same amount irrespective of whether you died 6 months or 6 years after the policy came into force.

Second, there is the *endowment policy*; the popularity and end-benefits of this type of policy have markedly declined, although many older policies are still current. Although it is not a life policy, it usually has a life element written in. For example, you take out an endowment policy for a lump sum to be paid to you in, say, 10, 15 or 20 years' time and for this a monthly premium is paid to the insurance company. That policy will, in most cases, have a death clause which says that if death occurs before the policy term has been completed a specifically stated sum of money will be paid out. If a policy had a with-profits element written into it, then this additional sum would also be paid out. This bonus of with-profits has had major setbacks, with amounts considerably reduced. Endowment policies themselves are not as popular as they used to be, mostly because the final figure at the end of the term in many instances does not meet the previously assumed sum.

Last, there is a *pensions policy*, which again, like the endowment policy, usually contains a death clause under which a payment is made if the policyholder dies after taking out the policy and before converting the pension fund into an annuity.

The Psychiatry Research Trust
needs Your help now.

Mental illness and brain disease can be devastating. They cause profound distress not only to their sufferers but also to their families and friends. No age is exempt - autism and hyperactivity in childhood, eating disorders, alcoholism and drug addiction in young adults, Motor Neurone Disease, Depression, Chronic Fatigue Syndrome in adults, Alzheimer's and Parkinson's disease in the elderly. Many more conditions affect individuals of all ages. Mental illness and brain disease are more common than many assume - they are part of everyone's life in some way

The Psychiatry Research Trust was formed in 1982 with the sole aim of raising funds for research at the Institute of Psychiatry, Bethlem and Maudsley hospitals.

Since that date the Trust has raised in excess of £12m which has been used to fund

advertisement feature

- research projects covering a wide spectrum of mental health conditions and brain disease
- lectures in aspects of mental health
- bursaries to enable students to study and also to carry out research projects
- prizes to encourage excellence in research by trainee psychiatrists and basic scientists
- the purchase of essential research equipment

This work is vital not only because it is directed at securing better treatment for sufferers but also because it seeks to understand the underlying causes of mental illness and brain disease with the aim of finding means of preventions and cures for these illnesses.

Scientists at the Institute of Psychiatry, Bethlem and Maudsley hospitals are seeking better ways of preventing and treating mental illness and brain disease. It will be more effectively treated and more easily prevented as long as the resources are available to fund essential research.

Your help is desperately needed.

The Psychiatry Research Trust only employs one full time and one part time staff members and therefore is able to keep its administrative costs to a minimum and the vast majority of all donations go directly to the research projects for which they have been given.

For further information or to make a donation, contact:

The Psychiatry Research Trust
PO87, De Crespigny Park
Denmark Hill, London SE5 8AF
Telephone: 0207 703 6217
Email: psychiatry_research_trust@kcl.ac.uk
Website: www.psychiatryresearch.org.uk
Registered Charity Number 284286

Stroke is the third biggest killer and the leading cause of severe adult disability in the UK.

A lasting gift in your Will to **The Stroke Association** will help us lead the fight against brain attacks.

To find out more about leaving a legacy and for details of our Free Will Scheme please call us on **020 7566 1505** or email **legacy@stroke.org.uk**

www.stroke.org.uk Stroke Helpline **0845 3033 100**

Stroke devastates lives – but with your help we are making a difference

Every five minutes, someone suffers their first stroke. Stroke does not discriminate – it can happen to anyone at any time of life.

For them and their family, life will never be the same again. Stroke kills 60,000 people a year across the UK and is the leading cause of severe adult disability.

A stroke is a brain attack. It happens when the blood supply to the brain is cut and brain cells die. Because the brain controls everything we do, think and feel – things we take for granted, like being able to move, balance, speak, understand, remember, see and hear – the brain damage caused by a stroke can be devastating. Yet for too long stroke provision has been inadequate and access to services that can make a difference between life and death, severe disability or manageable impairments, despair or hope has been something of a postcode lottery.

The Stroke Association is leading the fight against brain attacks. We are passionate about our vision of a world where there are fewer strokes and everyone affected by stroke gets the support they need. We are the only UK wide charity concerned with stroke in people of all ages. We fund research into prevention, treatment, better methods of rehabilitation and help stroke survivors and their families directly through our services such as Communication Support Group, Family and Carer Support Service, information services, welfare grants, publications and leaflets. The Stroke Association also campaigns, educates and informs to increase knowledge of stroke at all levels of society acting as a voice for everyone affected by stroke.

Little of this would be possible without those who remember us in their Will.

For information on how legacies help us soften the blow of stroke, contact the Legacy Department on **020 7566 1505** or email **legacy@stroke.org.uk**

Company pensions usually have a death clause which names a spouse or partner, or a child (children) under 18 years of age who in turn can receive part of the employee/pensionholder's pension pot should he or she die.

While annuities can be useful in providing income, they are also significant in inheritance tax planning, since when an annuity is purchased, the fund used to purchase it ceases to be an asset of the individual's estate. Instead regular payments are made to the annuitant (and perhaps his or her partner, depending on the type of annuity purchased) until death, when the payments cease unless any special arrangements were entered into before the purchase. Professional advice on this issue is therefore essential.

To realise money from an insurance policy, you have to produce the death certificate along with the policy documents, and, provided you are the beneficiary of that policy and can prove this, the money will be released. If not an indemnity form will need to be completed, signed and witnessed. Before sending all these documents off under registered post, do telephone the insurance company's head office asking for their specific requirements, and do remember to keep photocopies of all documents sent.

If you are a woman and over 45 when your husband dies, you will be able as a widow to claim a widow's pension, which is based upon your spouse's National Insurance contributions. The amount can be increased if you have children and they are under 19 and still in education but all payments cease with the child's portion of the benefit after they reach maturity. The amount of widow's pension must be included on your tax return as it forms part of your income. This benefit is known as widowed parent's allowance. A bereavement payment which is a non-taxable lump sum can also be applied for.

Inheritance tax has to be paid on an estate's value less allowable expenses once the threshold has been exceeded and before probate is granted, except, of course, where there is a direction that the estate is left to the surviving spouse. Although payment of this tax is due on a house or land or any interest held in a private firm, it can be deferred for up to six months from the end of the month in which death took place. The tax on this part of the estate may also be paid by instalments or by taking out a bank loan if there is no ready money in the estate. However, if the IHT due has not been paid by the end of this six-monthly period, interest is charged on a daily basis.

If you feel that either you (if you are the beneficiary of a close relation's will) or your close relatives (beneficiaries of your will) will not be able to meet the immediate charge of inheritance tax, you can take out a life policy to cover this provision provided you (or the beneficiaries) have an *insurable interest*. For example, a husband can take out this policy on his wife's life, or she on his, because a husband or his wife has an 'insurable interest', though this would seem to be paying out money for the sake of it, as if the wife/husband were the sole beneficiary then the estate would be exempt. If you are a single person and your brother, sister or parent is the sole beneficiary of your will, then that person may also be able to take out a policy on your life but they must have an insurable interest. If you are interested in knowing more, it is worth consulting an independent financial adviser (IFA) who should be able to recommend a suitable policy.

In life insurance, *term insurance* is the cheapest and it is best to shop around to find the best deal for you. Incidentally, the premium paid by women is less as they are considered to live longer. Non-smokers also pay less of a premium.

Whole of life is a more expensive life insurance as it guarantees a lump sum of money without stipulating a qualifying period. It also comes with a bonus option. Again, shop around for the deal best suited to your needs, using an IFA to advise you.

If you have life insurance as a means of paying inheritance tax, it is wise to keep abreast of your potential estate's value and the tax threshold to ensure adequate cover.

Whatever type of life policy you do decide to take out, remember that the interest from this policy's payout may provide the only income for your family's living expenses in your absence. Equate this with the cost of the insurance, and the term or period of time which it covers, and its affordability.

Consider what your financial input currently is and what it is likely to be. Next, consider what your family's current and future requirements are. How old are your children? What school are they currently at and will they be going on to higher education? Do not put the onus on to, say, your parents to provide for their grandchildren in the event of your death. This may not happen and it would leave your spouse trying to cope financially at a time of extreme stress.

Money

The definition of money in a will is taken to mean all cash held, including your loose cash, whether in a purse or wallet or hidden under the bed. It may also extend to a range of cash investment accounts, depending upon the context in which the will is written. These accounts range from National Savings accounts to bank and building society accounts and premium bonds. Gifts of money are termed *pecuniary legacies*.

For clarification, when making your will, use the term 'money' in its strict sense and refer to other financial assets, eg bank accounts, specifically.

Shares, unit trusts, Personal Equity Plans (PEPs), Individual Savings Plans (ISAs)

As the investment markets introduce new types of investment products, so these new investments may be bought by you and in turn find their way into your will. Shares, unit trusts, PEPs and ISAs can be disposed of just as if they were any other type of property given within the scope of your will. Share dividends sent after the owner's death also form part of the estate.

ISAs were introduced on 6 April 1999 as a continuance of the previous TESSAs and PEPs.

Once a person dies, then the ISA (PEP or TESSA) ceases to hold a tax-free status and is converted into an ordinary account, or unit trust, depending on the type of ISA held. From 6 April 2010, the ISA limits will increase from £3,600 for a cash ISA to £5,100 and for an equity ISA from £7.200 to £10,200. Investors over the age of 50 in tax year can take advantage from 6 November 2009 to benefit from this increase by increasing the amount held in an ISA for the 2009/10 tax year.

These assets will have to be valued as at the date of death. This subject is dealt with in detail in Chapter 10, Valuing and Administering the Estate.

However, if there is a life interest noted in your will, be very careful as to the wording of it in relation to the investment in unit trusts and shares as values can go down as well as up. In addition, the purchase of certain investments can actually produce a capital loss.

What is an executor? Who can be appointed?

An executor is a person who is named by you in your will to see that your wishes are carried out in accordance with the will, collect in the estate, pay any debts or expenses and then distribute the remainder to the named beneficiaries. Executors' duties commence immediately when death occurs and these duties cease once the estate has been distributed to the named beneficiaries.

You should always appoint someone to be the executor of your will. Before naming that person in your will it is best to ask him or her if he or she is willing to take on the duty. It is useful but not essential to appoint someone who has had previous business experience. Whoever is appointed, once the appointment is accepted, and actions taken in respect of the estate, he or she is obliged to carry out your exact wishes.

You may name as many executors as you wish but only four may be appointed to act by the Probate Registry at any one time. It is useful, though not essential, to name more than one person so that if one decides not to act there will still be someone else already appointed and familiar with your wishes. If only one executor is appointed and then turns down this role, the Probate Registry will apply the various rules and regulations to decide who should act in his or her place.

You can appoint a close friend or relative or a firm of solicitors, accountants or your bank to be the executor of your will. A minor or a person of unsound mind will not be allowed to act. Do be aware that if professionals agree to act, then a fee raised against the estate will be charged. This is called a charging clause and will have to be written into the will, stating that fees and expenses will be paid by the estate. Unless specified, a non-professional executor cannot charge a fee. There is nothing to prevent an executor from receiving a gift under the provisions laid out in the will but this gift will be seen to have been made on condition that he or she acts as executor, unless you state otherwise.

A private individual who acts as an executor and incurs expenses in carrying out those duties can claim back these expenses from the estate. However, he or she is not allowed to charge for time spent carrying out these duties. If, in an official capacity, an executor takes time off work and as a result loses money, then he or she is able to reclaim it from the estate as 'out of pocket' administration expenses.

If you have been appointed an executor but feel, for whatever reason, after the death that you cannot act, then you may renounce your executorship. You will be asked to sign a *form of renunciation* either by the Probate Registry or by the solicitor acting for other persons named in the will. Should you be holding the will but for some reason are unable to pass the document on to another interested person, then you may file the will at your nearest Probate Registry, signing a form stating that you do not, for whatever reason, wish to deal with the will. The Probate Registry will then appoint on application from another interested party a personal representative, usually the chief beneficiary of the will. The person thus appointed is known as the *administrator*.

A professional who has been named as one of your executors does not have an overriding right over other executors to administer your will. Each executor has an equal right to hold estate assets and apply for probate, with the agreement of all named executors. Joint applications can be made.

Where should a will be kept?

There is no legal obligation for you to register your will in any official office. This applies wherever you live in the United Kingdom. It is up to you to keep your will in a secure place and to inform your executors or your nearest relatives of its location, bearing in mind the original copy of the will needs to be kept in a safe, fire-proof location. If it is in a safe at home, then let the executor know the combination. If it is locked in a drawer, then let him or her have a key. Should you choose your solicitor or your bank to be one of the executors they will usually keep the will in their safe for you.

Wills can be deposited for safekeeping with the record keeper at the Probate Registry. You may do this through your local Registry or by calling at or writing to the Probate Dept, Principal Registry, Family Division, First Avenue House, 42–49 High Holborn, London WC1V 6NP. If you write to this office, a large envelope with instructions will be sent to you. All details asked for have to be noted, and it has to be signed and witnessed before being returned. Once the Probate Registry is in receipt of your will they will send you a deposit certificate. If you present the will personally they will hand the certificate over at that time. This certificate has to be produced by your executors after your death before the will is released to them.

The fee for keeping a will at First Avenue House is a nominal one-off charge. There are obvious advantages of doing it this way in that your executors know where the will is kept and you can rest assured that it is in one of the safest places. Also, in the event that a person is making an application to the Probate Registry and are unaware that a will exists, your will held at the

Registry can be matched to their application. The drawback is that should you wish to add a codicil to your will or make out a new one, you will have to produce the certificate before withdrawing the original will. The whole procedure will have to be gone through once again and a second fee would then be charged.

What is a trust?

It is not within the scope of this book to deal with the setting up of a trust; therefore the next few paragraphs are only a brief description.

If a trust is to be formed, you should ask a solicitor who specialises in trust matters to draw one up. However, if a minor is a beneficiary or if a life interest is given under the will then the will itself becomes a trust document. Remember that if a trust or life interest is to be included in a will, the costs to administer it can be expensive.

A trust would have been formed if the deceased felt that the beneficiaries would be better catered for by one; or if the beneficiaries are under the age of majority and their needs, both present and future, need careful administration; for tax reasons; or because the deceased felt that his or her estate should be passed on in perpetuity. However, it is not allowed to tie up a will, and the maximum period is now 'a life in-being plus 80 years'.

By creating a trust you place your estate (or part of it) in the hands of a person who is called a *trustee*. This person is appointed to a position of trust to carry out the provisions as expressed in the trust.

Before making the trust, ask the person whether he or she wishes to be a trustee. It is best to select at least two people to become trustees.

Trustees are legally bound to deal with the trust and its assets properly and to ensure that any beneficiary of the trust receives what is rightfully due to them.

As in the case of executorship, a trustee who is not a professional does not receive a specific payment for his or her time unless the trust stipulates to the contrary. Of course, expenses can be reclaimed from the trust. Naturally, professionals, whether they are banks, solicitors or accountants, will charge for their time and so you must be aware of what cost is likely to be incurred before creating the trust document.

There are a few points which you should be aware of if you are setting up a trust:

1. You cannot compel a person to act as a trustee.
2. A full inventory of the trust's property must be made at the outset.
3. If there is a life interest, it should state this fact in the trust and ensure that it gives the trustees power to look after whatever is included in the life interest, whether it is money, property, paintings, etc.
4. The trustees are legally bound to carry out the duty specified in the trust within the laws of the land.
5. Trustees are accountable for any neglect or default throughout the administration of the trust.

There have been instances where life tenants or beneficiaries of the trust have felt that they had been unjustly treated. Policing trusts is difficult and unless it can be proved that those involved in administering the trust have shown malice or that fraud has taken place, there is little that can be done. The role of trustee is a difficult one as the trustee must follow the trust's wishes absolutely but still balance the interests of the life tenant. Should anyone feel that they have been treated unjustly they should take proof of this to a solicitor, who in turn, if they feel it is justified, will write to the trustees in the hope of resolving matters.

In his 2006 Budget the Chancellor made radical changes to the tax structure relating to trusts. The first noticeable changes to accumulation and maintenance trusts were a few years ago, when the rate of tax increased from 34 per cent to 40 per cent. In the 2007 Budget the Chancellor introduced changes to all trusts, including those created by insurance policies and all trusts currently in existence. As far as accumulation and maintenance trusts are concerned, if a beneficiary does not receive his or her entitlement from the trust at the age of 18, then from the date the trust started for each 10-year period a tax charge of 4.2 per cent applies, provided that the trust sum exceeds the IHT threshold. It was also proposed to apply this charge to 'interest in possession' trusts, ie where a beneficiary has a legal right to all the trust's income (after tax and expenses) during his or her lifetime, but not to its property. (These are often used to provide a life income or life tenancy to a second wife, for example.) This charge where it applies to the wife has now been scrapped after considerable pressure from professional advisers. However, if the life tenant has a different relationship to the deceased, then tax applies. In the April 2009 Budget, the Chancellor announced a further increase to tax on discretionary trusts from 40 per cent to 50 per cent from 6 April 2010.

Small estates in England and Wales

Not to be confused with the definition applied in Scotland (see page 173), in England and Wales estates totalling £5,000 or less are considered to be small estates and a grant of probate or letters of administration may not be necessary.

Some institutions, such as banks, building societies and insurance companies, state that provided the sum involved is small they do not need a grant and that they can release the monies held once a release form has been drawn up. But be careful, for it is not as simple – or as cheap – as it first appears. First, there is often a charge levied for this, usually a minimum of £30, and second, a fee per asset is charged for a release document.

On the other hand, for personal applications as opposed to applications made by solicitors, to obtain a grant from the Probate Registry, no fee is charged for estates under £5,000; for those over £5,000 the fee is £90, with a charge of £1 per extra copy of the grant. While a release document is needed for each asset held by the various banks and insurance companies, only one grant of probate or letter of administration is needed and this document or official copies of it may be produced.

If, however, you do decide to use the service offered by these institutions, you will have to make a declaration on the release form, usually before a solicitor or magistrate; this has to be done each time you complete one of the forms. Again, a charge is levied on each occasion. In addition, it is often necessary for all benefiting persons to sign the release document, whereas if done through the Probate Registry only one or possibly two persons need to be involved with the procedure.

'Excepted estates'

Following successive increases to the value of excepted estates, the limit now stands at £312,000 of net chargeable estate for deaths on or after 6 April 2008, provided the application is made on or after 6 August 2008. This figure will rise from August 2009 to £325,000 of net chargeable estate for deaths on or after April 2009. This means that executors or administrators of straightforward estates will not have to supply the estate's accounts provided that the conditions noted on the following page have been met and that the value of the total gross estate has not exceeded £1,000,000. This limit applies to the aggregated gross value of the estate and of chargeable transfers of cash, quoted shares and securities within seven years before death. Excepted estates grant as mentioned here only refers to estates in England, Wales and Northern Ireland. HMRC claims that this increase will simplify the administration of 7,500 small estates per year with regard to inheritance tax.

Estates qualify as 'excepted estates' only if all the following conditions are met:

1. The total net chargeable value of the estate for tax purposes is not more than £325,000 (2009–10).

2. The estate comprises property that has passed under the deceased's will or intestacy or by nomination or by survivorship.[1]
3. Property outside the United Kingdom does not amount to more than £100,000 in value.
4. The deceased died domiciled in the United Kingdom and had not made lifetime gifts which would have been chargeable to inheritance tax.
5. The total gross value of chargeable transfers of cash, quoted shares or securities within seven years *before* death has been introduced at a value of £150,000. If the estate includes any assets held in trust then these assets should be in one single trust with a gross value up to £150,000.

Estates do not qualify if the deceased had made a 'chargeable potentially exempt transfer' or had made a gift with 'a reservation that subsists at the time of death or within seven years of the death'. However, it is allowable for assets up to £100,000 to be held in a trust. Lastly, estates will not qualify if the deceased had an interest in settled property. These changes do not affect Scotland.

What is a life interest?

Before making a will you would need to decide whether or not you hold the type of asset that can be left in a life interest, for example a house or interest from your investments. A life interest allows you to let an individual have the use of your house or interest from your investments without being left these absolutely; in other words, without any conditions. If you decide on giving a life interest in the property to your spouse, then your spouse would benefit from its use for the

---

[1] If the value of an estate is attributable in part to property which passes by survivorship in joint tenancy, then it is the value of the deceased's beneficial interest in that property that is taken into account for the purpose of valuation and the IHT threshold.

rest of his or her life, passing it on to other stated beneficiaries under the terms of your will upon death. Life interest in a property, for example, would mean that your spouse could live in or rent the property for the rest of his or her life but would not actually own it.

House repairs and maintenance would obviously need to be carried out at some time, so it would have to be decided by you and stated in your will whether the life interest beneficiary would pay for this or whether it would be paid for jointly by all the beneficiaries concerned. Rentals earned would go directly to the person who is benefiting from the life interest should the property be rented to another individual.

If the life interest involves money, your spouse would receive the interest that the capital sum earned but the capital and any capital growth if so indicated would remain intact for the other beneficiaries upon his or her death as directed in their will. You would need to decide on the amount of acceptable interest, capital growth, or a mixture of both. Your decision would need to be included in your will or given in a letter enclosed with your will. For stocks and shares, the life interest would entitle your spouse to the receipt of income (interest and dividends) but not the actual capital invested. Do specify the type of investment as otherwise it will be left to the discretion of the trustees.

The benefit of life interest is that your surviving spouse has the house and income for life and the children benefit thereafter. You direct who receives what. However, there is a downside to it. First, your personal representative is not able to finalise the administration of the estate until the life interest ceases, and second, a life interest can be expensive to administer. Income tax forms, trust accounts and so on will have to be completed annually and perhaps a financial adviser brought in too. All these experts will charge fees for handling matters. The only other way would be to stipulate one type of investment to produce income, the other type to produce capital growth, and to ensure that your spouse receives all income. This would then go on his or her tax return and he or she would complete the trust tax return also. On the death of the life tenant, the value of the life interest would have to be added into the life tenant's estate for calculation of IHT. Unless your estate is of sufficient size and value to warrant it, or you feel your children's rights should be safeguarded above everything in case your spouse remarries, a life interest should not be considered.

Absolute gift is simpler as it means leaving outright any possession you direct without stipulation to the named beneficiary. In fact this alternative is the more common, and cheaper, of the two, but in this case it is not possible for you to be certain that your original beneficiary will pass on the estate in the way you prefer.

Overseas property

An increasing number of people have purchased a second home abroad, or are the fortunate recipient through inheritance.

Should you be domiciled and deemed domiciled in the UK then the value of that overseas property is included in the value of your total estate, ie worldwide assets. Some countries require you to make a will before a notary when you become the owner of a property in their country (eg Spain), and depending on the value of the property, the tax rules of the IHT in that country and whether or not it is jointly owned, it may mean that you have IHT to pay in that country. There is an international tax agreement, which the UK is a signatory to, for income and capital gains tax and for most countries for IHT also, which means that if you pay IHT in the country which holds such an agreement then the tax paid on the asset can be offset against the IHT due in the UK on your total estate.

It is therefore important to organise your affairs taking this property's value and any overseas bank account into your overall planning.

As far as your UK will is concerned, you should acknowledge ownership of these overseas assets with wording to the effect 'this Will does not relate to my immoveable property in [*country*] or [*outside England and Wales*] which is subject to a separate will [if that is the case] made according to the law of that country'.

4

What Can Affect Your Will?

There are three ways in which your will can be revoked or made inoperable. The first two are deliberate acts through choice. You can destroy your will or you can make a new will that includes a statement that you wish to revoke the earlier document. The third one applies in England and Wales: if you get married and have not specifically stated in your will that after this event you wish your current will to remain in force, your marriage will invalidate the will.

Marriage

Let us take the unconscious act of invalidating a will; that is, through marriage. Scottish readers should see page 182 for the application of Scottish law. In England and Wales, to avoid revoking your will by marriage, you can insert a statement to the effect that the will is to remain effective after your marriage to a specifically 'named' person. If you do this, the will is not revoked when you marry. So if you expect to marry a particular person at the time the will is made, then provided the following clause is inserted, any such will would still remain valid. But remember, you must name the person you intend to marry.

Example

'I [name] make this will in contemplation of my marriage to [name] and wish this will to remain in force after the said marriage.'

Divorce

If you divorce, under English law, then from the date of the decree absolute your former husband or wife will no longer benefit from your will and any gift made to him or her will lapse or be void. Should the former spouse be an executor and/or trustee, this appointment would fail if the will predated the divorce. The rest of the will is not revoked, and gifts to other persons remain effective. Unless you have made proper alternative provisions in your will to cover this eventuality the subject of the gift will be dealt with as if you had died intestate and may not pass in the manner that you would have wished. Moreover, it is possible that your ex-partner will administer the estate – in the role of guardian – on your children's behalf.

Your spouse is also entitled to half of any inheritance you may receive up until the date of your decree absolute. Thereafter, under English law, they are not entitled to receive a share unless specified in the will.

Revocation of a will

The making of a new will usually revokes a previous one provided a statement to this effect is placed in the will, namely 'I revoke all former wills and testamentary dispositions previously made by me.' Even if this statement is not included there will be an implied revocation of earlier wills if the later document clearly disposes of the whole estate.

Another instance where a will is naturally revoked is if it is deliberately physically destroyed by the person who has written it with the intention of revoking it. A will can also be destroyed by another person on the instructions of the testator but this must be done in his or her presence and under his or her direction, and the testator must intend that the will is to be revoked by such destruction. If this happens, the testator must categorically state to the third person present that it is his or her intention to destroy and revoke the will and then instruct that person to do so on his or her behalf.

Writing across the top of your will 'I revoke this will' does not mean that the will ceases to exist. You can, of course, accidentally destroy a will by destroying your own signature or that of your witnesses but unless the intention was there to revoke the will, legally it remains valid and unrevoked.

If a codicil accompanies a will and you later revoke that will by destruction, unless you also destroy the accompanying codicil it remains in force.

Legally, you cannot unintentionally destroy your will. If you lose it while moving house, the will is still considered to be legally in force and only by making out a new will revoking its predecessor will the old one be made void.

An example of assumed destruction of a will is if your executors cannot find it after your death although it is known that one had been made. If it was last known to have been in your possession, there is a legal presumption that it has been revoked by you. This presumption can be rebutted by evidence showing that there was definitely no intention to revoke the will.

Attestation clause

As important as a revocation clause is the attestation clause. It confirms that you are the testator and that you have agreed this will and signed it in the presence of witnesses who themselves have signed it in your presence. A faulty attestation clause (or the absence of one) does not invalidate a will. But in such circumstances the Probate Registry will require evidence to confirm that the will was signed and attested correctly. This is especially relevant if the testator is blind or partially sighted, in which case the clause has to state that the will was read to the person and the person agreed and appeared to understand the will before signing it. Some wills have the blind and partially sighted clause at the foot of the will and then this is signed once more by the testator and witnesses.

A 'wish of intent'

To the best of human endeavours, the State intends that the persons named in your will should benefit from your property, according to the terms of your will. However, if the language of the will is ambiguous, then further investigation by the executor or, in some instances, the court may be called for. Evidence would have to be shown in order to try to interpret your wishes. This evidence can take the form of letters sent to your next of kin or conversations held with them when you expressed a 'wish of intent' or actions that indicate unchanged affection. They would have to swear that this was exactly what happened, however. Any falsification of evidence would be a serious matter indeed. This is why it is so important to express clearly what your intentions are.

Disputes and unknown factors

Suppose Great Uncle Harry dies without any issue, leaving you as his only descendant. If you had an argument and he decided not to leave you a legacy, under the Inheritance (Provision for Family and Dependants) Act 1975, you are able to apply to the court to be given part of Great Uncle Harry's estate. However, you would first have to establish that you were in some way a dependant of his. The court's powers are wide and in order to stand a chance of receiving any inheritance under the Act's provisions you would have to show that you were materially supported by him; for example, he supported you financially, he let you live under his roof, gave you food and made sure that you were physically well cared for.

A further example of unknown factors overturning the wishes of a will is if you divorced and later married a divorcee who had a child. Then if you and your new wife in turn had a child and you forgot or intentionally failed to name either in your will, they would be able to put a claim in against your estate as they could be seen to be 'children of the family' and therefore dependants. Again, it is up to the discretion of the court to decide on the proportion of the estate, if any, to be paid out.

Another common wish inserted in wills that can cause disputes is one of continuous family inheritance. It has a moral implication rather than a legal one because of the Statute of Limitations, which allows a maximum of a 'life in being' plus 80 years. This is also the length of time for which copyright persists after the death of the creator of an original work (an author, composer etc), so the clause is often used to indicate what the person wishes to be done with the continuing royalty income from the work. Also, you cannot dictate what another person does with his or her will. In cases such as this, you can make a gift of a life interest only to be passed back to the estate upon death and then on to the next stated beneficiary.

Although it would not make your will invalid if you state in it that you wish your eldest child to have a certain item and in turn he or she is requested to pass this item on to his or her eldest child, it might not occur. So despite the fact that they are under a moral duty to do this, there is no legal obligation.

You cannot stipulate in your will that your house must be lived in by your son if it inflicts separation between parent and child or instigates the intention of breaking up a marriage. Such clauses are deemed to be 'contrary to public policy' and the law ensures that such stipulations do not stand. The same applies to religion. You cannot stipulate in your will that your grandchildren (or any other person named in your will) be brought up in a particular religious faith in order to inherit from your estate. To insert a clause stating that a child will be excluded from a legacy if he or she is brought up in a religion other than his or her own would be to invalidate that section of your will. Again, it is seen as contrary to public policy. The definition of a specific religion is also seen as too vague and extensive clarification would be needed.

The term 'contrary to public policy' can be seen in many different ways and nowadays will often be discarded because the phrase itself is too vague. It is supposed to reflect what is believed to be public policy at the present time.

Courts can, once petitioned, examine the disposition of gifts within the will if those gifts are regarded as 'contrary to public policy'. However, in such instances it is up to the court on the day to decide on the individual merit of each case. Therefore, it is not possible to expand further within the terms of this book. A solicitor experienced in probate matters should be consulted where such a situation arises.

Claiming against an estate

Claims against an estate do happen from time to time when a will is unclear or if the holdings of the deceased did not belong to him or her. Other reasons for challenging a will could be where a parent promised, say, the businesses in which the child had worked with the parent, to that child, but then for whatever reason the parent changed his or her mind and resettled that part of the estate, thereby depriving the child of his or her livelihood. A will may also be successfully challenged on the basis of its not being valid if the deceased was deemed not to have testamentary capacity when he or she signed the will.

The circumstances under which a claim against an estate might be made are too numerous to mention, but fortunately many are settled out of court. In the first instance, you should go to a solicitor who specialises in probate matters or to the Citizens' Advice Bureau in order to ascertain the merits of your case. Remember the court cannot give you advice as it is there to make a judgment on your claim.

If you continue to pursue the claim then a probate claims form has to be obtained from the Chancery Court or one of the larger County Courts that deals with Chancery matters. This form needs to be completed to include information about yourself and each defendant, namely the capacity in which you are claiming and in which the defendant is being sued. The claim form must contain a statement of the interest of the claimant and why you intend to question the terms of the will when it was executed.

This form must then be signed by you or your solicitor or 'litigation friend'. Contempt of court can be brought against any statement of truth made without an 'honest belief in that truth'. A copy of the will together with the statement and any written evidence in support of the claim will need to be sent to the court.

It cannot be stressed too much that before this process commences, the applicant must consider very carefully the financial and emotional costs such actions can result in. It is not unheard of for the bulk if not all of the estate to be lost through legal charges.

Making a gift void

Wills may be declared invalid if it is proved that they were made as a result of excessive pestering, in other words if someone tried to persuade you to leave everything you own (or even a specific gift) to them. So, if a person has imposed undue influence on you, and this can be proved, the will can be seen as invalid.

If a murder was committed by a beneficiary of a will (or indeed the beneficiary aided and abetted somebody in causing the death of the testator), regardless of the benefits noted in the will the murderer or accomplice would receive no inheritance. In committing the crime he or she automatically forfeits his or her right to inherit.

A condition attached to a gift in the will that requires the beneficiary to commit an unlawful act of whatever nature is not recognised and the gift will usually be paid without regard to the condition. Of course, whether this is a statement in a will or not, the request is illegal.

You should not ask a beneficiary or the spouse of a beneficiary to witness your will because in so doing you are making the gift void.

Overall, it should be remembered that although any related party can challenge a will, generally, unless a person has a valid claim, for example, lack of testamentary capacity, or undue influence, the courts do not as a rule turn aside the testator's wishes. The invalidation of your will, therefore, is not a matter that should worry you unduly providing you sign before two witnesses and they sign at the same time.

Rules to follow

To ensure that you make a valid will there are a few rules to follow. First, you must be over 18 years of age, and second, you must sign the will in the presence of two witnesses both of whom must be present at the same time. Those witnesses must then, before leaving your presence, sign their names at the bottom of the document and it is useful for them to note their addresses although not essential. There is another requirement. You must also be mentally capable of understanding your actions and know what you are doing, and intending to do, when signing your will. If a solicitor has been used, he or she is legally obliged to have satisfied himself or herself that you were mentally competent and understood what you were signing.

There is an exception to the age requirement noted above. A person over 14 but under 18 can make a will, provided that the person is on active military service in times of war. Similarly, seamen at sea in peacetime may also exercise this privilege.

It cannot be stressed too often that a will must clearly state your intentions, in other words exactly who is to receive precisely what. Many a confusion occurs and many a will is made invalid because the instructions are not clear.

'All my property' means just that – absolutely everything you own. You might have wanted the house to go to your spouse and perhaps some of your personal effects; also, you may have wanted a few mementoes to go to your son, mother or friend. With the use of the above phrase, they would receive nothing.

Another stumbling block when a will is being written by a layperson is the over-indulgent use of what are considered to be legal phrases. Again, you may think you meant one thing but, in fact, it would be judged as something entirely different. For example, 'I leave all my money' means 'I leave you all my cash', nothing else, just cash in its physical form and in bank and building society accounts. It does not include the value of the house, furnishings or any other valuable you own or, indeed, even the value that any such items could realise. Keep the phrases simple and specific, and select your words carefully.

The main tasks of the Probate Registry are to decide on the validity of a will and to interpret it for the purpose of deciding who to appoint as personal representatives. Unclear statements can cause problems when it comes to making this interpretation. In 1988 new Non-Contentious Probate Rules were introduced giving the Registrar some discretion as to enquiries that could be made with regard to establishing the validity of a will. This book cannot possibly cover all these considerations, whether or not you have written the will yourself. If you are unsure as to its correctness then you should check to make sure that your will has been prepared correctly.

Basically, the Registrar cannot alter the distribution arrangements as laid out in the will. However, if it becomes clear that there has been some mistake in the wording made by the person writing the will on behalf of the testator, because of a misunderstanding, the Registrar may, on behalf of the testator, put the mistake right provided all persons affected by this action agree to it. However, the will's intentions cannot be altered: so if monies are given, then all cash is inherited; if a house is given, then the property is passed on; and if 'all that I own' is given, then everything the deceased owned must be passed on. Of course, if a spouse, son or daughter, or, indeed, any person who claims to be a dependant, is excluded, they can apply to the court and ask to be awarded part of the estate. Then it is up to the court to decide the validity of the claim.

A will is accepted as valid in England and Wales without query if it appears to be signed properly and has a clause called an *attestation clause* inserted in it. (Printed wills obtained from stationers have this clause.) This clause confirms that the necessary rules have been followed when a person signs the will. If it has not been inserted, enquiries will usually have to be made to confirm that the will was properly signed.

In England and Wales an unwitnessed will is invalid but in Scotland (see Chapter 11) a *holograph* (written in the person's own hand) will is not necessarily invalid merely because it is not witnessed. Alterations made to a will after it has been properly signed will not take effect unless the will is signed and witnessed again. Sometimes minor alterations do occur and provided that this happens before the will is signed, the incorrect word or line should be crossed out and the substitute one written above it. At the time the will is signed and witnessed you should place your initials alongside the altered text. The witnesses must also place their initials alongside the alterations. Do not erase incorrect words.

The best rule to follow, however, should be that if alterations are necessary, then make out a new will. Only minor alterations should be inserted in the form of a codicil. A codicil acts as an insertion in your will; for example, the amended distribution of a particular item.

It does not matter what your will has been written on provided that the Registrar sees that it is a fair copy. Registrars are used to receiving all manner of wills, from those written on brown paper to, on occasions, those written on tracing paper – although such a presentation is not recommended.

5

How to Write a Will

One of the greatest problems facing the Probate Registry is unclear meaning in the wording in many 'home-made' wills. While there is sufficient leeway for the Registrar to make an interpretation, in some cases this is not possible and the will then has to have its meaning defined in accordance with the rules, possibly in a higher court, namely the Chancery Court. The courts try to decipher what the deceased may have wanted to say, but a precise interpretation may not be possible because of the unclear wording. Any ambiguity, whether in the usage of a word or a phrase, must be avoided. This rule applies even if a solicitor is drawing up your will as it has been known for them to make mistakes too. For example, a gift of your possessions held 'in' your property means held in your abode, while held 'in and on' means both in the house and on the property's plot. If prepared for you, then read your will to ensure it says what you mean to happen.

When writing your will you must state clearly, using full names, who is to receive the gift as well as giving a full description of the item or items named. For example, if you have two antique button-back chairs and you want your favourite niece to receive one, then describe the chair precisely. Give the colour of the upholstery, trim and any small detail that can help in identifying the chair, and your niece's full name and current or last known address.

Before writing your will or deciding on any IHT planning, do consider any dependants you have and how any of your proposed plans may affect them. For example, by saving IHT and leaving half your share of the house or your money to another member of your family, you may in turn leave your surviving spouse in a difficult financial or legal position.

Checklist for your will

On a separate sheet of paper you should note what assets you have and whom you wish to benefit. When looking at the valuation of your estate (see the checklist, Example 1, pages 72–73), make sure that it is not going to attract more inheritance tax than at first anticipated or indeed Capital Gains Tax in certain capital items put in trust. If it is, you should take steps to examine how this liability can be lessened (see Chapters 6 and 7).

You will need to state in your will whether your individual beneficiaries have to pay inheritance tax from their legacy or whether you wish all legacies to be paid in full and any tax due to be taken out of the balance of the residue of the estate. If you have any outstanding debts, perhaps a loan from the bank or a mortgage, this should also be noted in your lists so that your calculations of these debts can be deducted from its total. These debts are deducted from the value of your estate before calculating your inheritance tax liability. Remember, whatever route you decide to take, tax usually has to be paid before probate is granted. Prior to the amendment in the Banking Act, a loan could be obtained from a bank to raise the tax money and the interest from the loan could be deducted from the estate's value when calculating the total inheritance tax liability. However, although this route speeds up the process in that the grant may be obtained quickly, it is not the best route to take as the interest still has to be paid and, although deducted from tax due, it is not 100 per cent relievable, ie you still pay 40 per cent in the pound. Another route for payment of tax is if the estate holds any National Savings monies or premium bonds, and this now extends to bank and building society accounts; then your solicitor, or, if you are making a personal application, the Probate Registry, can organise with these authorities for the tax to be deducted from such holdings.

While we are on the subject of loans, if you have given a loan to another person and it is meant to be repaid but at the time of your death it has not been, then the value of that loan outstanding at the time of death must be added back into your estate to arrive at the taxable total of your estate. You may have wished the residue at death to be treated as a gift and provided that was made clear and seven years has elapsed then it is not added back into your estate. If a loan was given by you and interest was charged on that loan then it would be up to you to declare the additional income earned. Failure to do so would result in penalties and interest charges against you, or, if deceased, then your estate.

Case study

Mr A. N. Other is married and aged 42. He lives with his wife and two children, both minors. He has his own home, in joint names with his wife, with a mortgage of £90,000, also in joint names. Both Mr and Mrs A. N. Other's parents are still alive and both Mr and Mrs Other have siblings. The couple are also employed. Mr A. N. Other dies.

This is a typical case. What should he have done to ensure adequate protection for both his wife and his children? The important point to note here is that both parents should have in their respective wills clear instructions as to the guardianship of their children should both parents die. There might be a separate guardian document in place. In the case of a divorce these arrangements would have to have been made clear. If the Others' house was owned by them jointly as tenants in common, then if Mr Other's half share caused his estate to exceed the IHT threshold, and it was left to any person other than his wife (transfers between spouses are exempt from IHT), IHT would be payable on Mr Other's death assuming his estate was over the IHT threshold.

In death, Mr Other would be leaving a 'young' family in need of all the financial help it could muster; therefore, the best solution in this case would be to leave the estate to his wife but perhaps put a small provision in the names of the children (taking note of the changes in trust law: see pages 52–54).

However, had Mr Other died 10 years later, having inherited from his parents' estates, he would have a larger estate to distribute. Mr Other has been a fortunate man and has received an inheritance. This inheritance came from an estate where no IHT had been paid. It has added £100,000 to his estate making his total gross estate £455,650. Should he leave all of his estate to his wife then it is free of IHT due to the spousal exemption, but Mrs Other would pay tax on the portion of her estate over the IHT threshold on her death, and as of 9th October 2007 the unused portion of her late husband's IHT threshold, assuming she has not remarried and left a portion of her estate to her new husband Q. Mr Other could consider leaving his half share of the property to Mrs Other as a life tenant, and if circumstances allowed, leave a portion up to the IHT threshold to his children in trust. CGT on the transfer to the children at the age specified in the will may produce CGT implications. But as the IHT threshold is currently only £325,000 this may present a dilemma of financial feasibility. It may be that in these circumstances adequate insurance should be examined.

Below is an example of preplanning which Mr A. N. Other may do. Once this preplanning stage is done, he will be able to draft his own will.

For a more comprehensive list of items for inclusion see the Estate Checklist in Chapter 11, pages 177–78.

Example 1. Checklist of assets of A. N. Other

Item			Amount £
House	value	£320,000	
	less mortgage	£90,000	
	half share		115,000
Life insurance with [name] Co Ltd			
	on death worth		60,000

Pension with [name] Co Ltd on death worth	44,000
Current value of shares and unit trusts held	5,000
Building society accounts	
[name] Building Society (1)	1,500
[name] Building Society (2)	1,900
Bank accounts with [name] deposit	750
Second-hand value of car	7,500
Half of furnishings and personal effects (resale value)	5,000
Approximate total	£240,650

Example 2. Notes for legacy in [name] will

1. My wife, [name], is to have the house, car, money in the building society and bank accounts [names and account numbers], furnishings except for those listed below, half the proceeds of my life insurance policy with [insurance company's name] and the residue of my estate.
2. My children, [name] and [name], to receive half of the proceeds of my life insurance with [insurance company's name] to be held in trust with my wife as trustee.
3. To my brother, [name], half of the value of my shares and unit trusts and my Hornby train set.
4. To my mother, [name], half of the value of my shares and unit trusts and my gold fob watch with chain.
5. To my friends, [name] and [name], the gate-legged oak table with inlaid top.
6. If my wife dies before me, ask my brother, [name], to set up a trust and act on the children's behalf until they reach the age of 18. [State who your children's guardian will be].

Before moving on to the writing of a will and different examples of clauses that can be inserted, it is worth noting that you are able to purchase a printed will form from any of the large high street stationers. However, there is not a great deal of space allowed for the provision of various legacies and additional sheets would have to be inserted.

'I should never have switched from Scotch to Martinis'

These were believed to be Humphrey Bogart's last words, but it was his wife, Lauren Bacall, whose words said the final goodbye. In his urn she placed a small gold whistle inscribed: 'If you need anything, just whistle', the immortal line she delivered to Bogart in 'To Have and Have Not', their first film together. We all have our own way of saying goodbye, but if we all did it by leaving a gift to charity as well as our family in our wills we could make a huge difference. Otherwise, most charities will struggle to survive and that's one farewell the world can do without. **Make your last wishes something to remember.**

Registered charity England and Wales (no. 1079573) and Scotland (no. SC038971).

REMEMBER A CHARITY IN YOUR WILL
Help the work live on...

Call 020 7840 1030 or visit
rememberacharity.org.uk/press

It's a common myth that only the rich and famous leave money to charity when they die. This couldn't be any further from the truth. The reality is without the gifts left in wills by people like you, many of the charities we know and support today wouldn't even exist.

Legacies are the foundation for many charities in the UK and are vital in making sure that all the good work they do can continue.

Thankfully 74%* of the UK population support charities and when asked, 35% of people say they'd happily leave a gift in their will once family and friends have been provided for.

The problem is only 7% actually do.

That's why, if we all leave some money in our wills to charity as well as our family, we can make a huge difference. In fact, if we can raise this figure to just 11% we would create an additional £1 billion for charities in the UK every year, which would ensure that their work lives on.

So, you don't have to be rich and famous to make a difference. We can all do something amazing for the world just by leaving a gift in our wills to charity.

For more information about Remember A Charity and how to leave a gift in your will, please go to
www.rememberacharity.org.uk

* TNS Social 2008

THE PARKINSON'S DISEASE SOCIETY

Dedicated to supporting all people with Parkinson's Disease, their families, friends and carers.

Parkinson's disease does not discriminate and can affect anyone at any age. Public figures such as Muhammad Ali and the actor Michael J. Fox both have the illness. The condition is a progressive, neurological disorder and occurs when the chemical messenger responsible for movement stops being produced in the brain. Medication and other treatments mean that many people with Parkinson's can continue to lead an active life but others can have their quality of life affected dramatically.

The Parkinson's Disease Society (PDS) is a registered charity, founded in 1969 by Mali Jenkins, whose sister had Parkinson's. The Society is celebrating its 40th year this year and now has more than 29,000 members, 40,000 supporters and over 330 branches and support groups throughout the UK.

What do we do?

We provide support, advice and information to everyone affected by Parkinson's disease including health and social services professionals involved in the management and care of Parkinson's. Each year the PDS commits more than £4m to funding research into the cause, cure and prevention of Parkinson's, and improvements in available treatments. The Society works to campaign and influence Government policy and the development of high-quality services at a local and national level, including the education of professionals working with people with Parkinson's.

We believe all people with Parkinson's should have access to high-quality and integrated health and social care services delivered by professionals with a good understanding of the condition wherever they live across the UK.

What help is available?

The PDS has a wide range of information booklets, leaflets and DVDs available for everyone affected by Parkinson's. There is a range of publications for professionals working with people with Parkinson's, with many of these resources available for free. We have a network of Information and Support Workers for Parkinson's and run a dedicated freephone helpline (0808 800 0303) staffed by specialist nurses which offers advice and support to anyone affected by the condition and also produces a wide range of information on all aspects of living with Parkinson's, including treatments for the condition, welfare and benefits and advice on living with Parkinson's at a younger age.

Where do we work?

In addition to a national office based in London, the PDS has a large number of field staff who work to improve the lives of people with Parkinson's in their local area. PDS branches exist across the UK and offer people with Parkinson's, their carers, families and friends support and information. To find your nearest branch please call 020 7932 1338 or visit our website.

How are we funded?

As a charity, we are entirely reliant on voluntary donations to deliver our services. With your support, we can reach out to more people with Parkinson's, their carers and families, and fund research that may one day lead to an effective cure. Over half of our income comes from gifts in wills and without these gifts, much of our work would not have been possible. An informative Will Making Guide is available, free of charge, to anyone who is interested in leaving a legacy.

How can I get involved?

If you would like to become a member of the PDS, please contact the membership team on 020 7932 1344. Membership costs just £4 a year for UK residents and you will receive our quarterly magazine The Parkinson. All our members have the right to attend the Society's Annual General Meeting and you can also get involved in the running of your local branch if you wish to. If you would like to receive more information, make a donation or are considering leaving a gift to the PDS in your Will, please contact us using the details below.

Parkinson's Disease Society,
215 Vauxhall Bridge Road,
London, SW1V 1EJ
Tel: 020 7931 8080
Fax: 020 72339908
Helpline: 0808 800 0303
Email: enquiries@parkinsons.org.uk
Web: www.parkinson.org.uk
Charity registered in England and Wales No. 258197
and in Scotland No. SCO37554.

Every three minutes someone is diagnosed with diabetes. Every three minutes, someone's life changes forever.

With the number of people with diabetes growing year on year, there has never been a more urgent need for funding. Will you help them by remembering Diabetes UK in your will?

By leaving a gift to Diabetes UK in your will today, you can improve the lives of people with diabetes – today, tomorrow and in the years ahead. Call **0845 123 2399** or email **legacies@diabetes.org.uk** for more information.

The charity for people with diabetes
Macleod House, 10 Parkway, London NW1 7AA
A charity registered in England and Wales (no.215199) and in Scotland (no. SCO39136)

FundRaising
Standards Board

A Hope For The Future

For over 75 years Diabetes UK has provided help and support for people with diabetes, as well as to their family, friends and carers. Our mission remains to improve the lives of people with the condition and work towards a future without diabetes. Crucial to us achieving this is your support of:

- Our Careline which answered over 35,000 queries from people with diabetes in 2008
- Our Care Event Holidays which give more than 250 children each year the opportunity to learn how to manage their diabetes and meet other children with this condition
- Our vast range of publications which provide the latest news and advice for people of all ages and stages living with diabetes

advertisement feature

One way in which you can support the vital work of Diabetes UK is by leaving a gift in your will. The idea that your hopes, beliefs and values can be encapsulated in this one document is inspiring. As the largest charity for people with diabetes, we are immeasurably grateful to those individuals who chose to remember us in this way. Much of our work is only possible because of people who care deeply about this debilitating condition and want to ensure their support continues through their will.

Naturally, family and loved ones must come first and there is great peace of mind from knowing those you care about most will be taken care of. But once those provisions are made, did you know that even a fraction of what's left can be immensely valuable to Diabetes UK?

Our greatest hope is that one day, we will find a cure for diabetes. It may not happen in this lifetime but there will be life-changing breakthroughs in treatments and prevention to be made along the way.

If you would like any more information on the work of Diabetes UK or how to go about leaving a gift in your will to charity, you can request a free copy of our will guide to help you. Simply contact our Legacy Manager on:

Telephone: 020 7424 1000
Email: legacies@diabetes.org.uk
Web: www.diabetes.org.uk/legacy

Become a legacy Pioneer by remembering a gift to Diabetes UK in your will. Thank you

advertisement feature

When writing your own will there is one clause that must always be included. Many a new will is written and the old one is forgotten or ignored. The phrase which should be inserted in every new will is, 'I revoke all former wills and codicils and testamentary provisions.' If you make a new will forgetting to destroy the earlier one, and if this *revocation clause* is not included, the later will may not prevail in its entirety. On occasions when this happens both documents may have to be proved and the combined provisions, provided they are not inconsistent with each other, are applied.

Always keep a carbon copy or a photocopy of your will whether it is handwritten or typed. Do ensure that your executor(s) know its location. Always advise your executors of any change.

The following checklist of sentences appears in sequence in any will. The letters at the start of each sentence refer to the example of a will to be found on pages 84–87 and to further inclusions which are found on pages 87–91.

(A)   A will should always start with the sentence 'This is the last will and testament of [name]'.

(B)   This statement is followed by your full name, your full current address and the date that the will is being made.

(C)   A statement revoking all previous wills and codicils and testamentary provisions is inserted next.

(D)   A statement appointing your executors and noting whether any payment is to be made to them is needed. If you are a parent of a child or children who are minors and you have not already documented an appointment of a guardian in the event of your death, then at this point in your will this should be done.

(E)   If you have any particular wishes, such as funeral arrangements, these wishes should be inserted next.

(F)   A statement needs to be included to the effect that all estate expenses incurred (known as *testamentary expenses*) should be paid by the estate. Also this section should state whether the gifts made in the will are to be free of inheritance tax liability. If this is the case, you will have to allow for the correct amount when first preparing your estate valuation.

(G) Now you list any specific gifts of money (known as *pecuniary legacies*) in detail, stating who is to receive what amount. The following statement should be made for each gift: 'I give and bequeath the following legacy to [name] of [address].' If you wish these legacies to be paid from a particular fund you should state this by inserting 'payable from my deposit account in [name] Bank plc'. Note, however, that should you close this account, the legacy will not be paid from another source; or if a car has been given as a gift in the will but sold prior to your death a replacement for this gift will not be made, unless you specifically make a statement to this effect.

(H) After (G), the following statement listing other legacies is inserted for each gift: 'I give and bequeath the following to [name] of [address].' Note carefully what gift is to be received and if it is, say, a house or a piece of land, then note the exact location.

(I) You should end your will with a clause disposing of those assets that you have not as yet given to anyone. The *residue* or remainder of the estate would go to this person (or persons) once all debts (inheritance tax, funeral expenses and so on) have been paid. A suitable clause would be: 'I devise and bequeath the residue of my real and personal estate.' In addition, a *survivorship clause* should be inserted stating that should this main beneficiary not survive you by 30 days [or such period as you wish to specify] the residue of the estate should go to another named person. This is done to clarify any possible claim by beneficiaries from either side should, for example, both husband and wife die in the same accident where the precise time of death could not be established. If the husband died in an accident and 10 days later his main beneficiary, ie his wife, also died, the residue of his estate which was being left to her would go to his other substituted chief beneficiary. Without this clause the husband's estate would have been given across to his wife's estate for distribution according to the bequests of her will or the rules of intestacy governing her estate.

(J)   The last line of your wishes is followed by what is known as the *attestation clause*: 'Signed by the said testator in the presence of us present at the same time and by us in his [or her] presence.' Here you may sign either beside the clause or below it and the signatures of your two witnesses also appear here, below your signature. Each witness should also write his or her full current address. (Remember, neither a beneficiary of the will nor the spouse of a beneficiary may witness the will. In such an event, the gift is forfeit.)

As individual needs and circumstances differ, so each will and its content will reflect these differences. A married man with a wife and child will want to ensure that they are well provided for. An elderly person who has no close relatives would perhaps want to leave his or her estate not only to relatives but to charity or friends. A single person, with perhaps a brother or sister, will have different priorities and the same would apply to a widow or widower. The sample will that follows allows for the adoption of different clauses which different people may want to include. The letters in brackets relate to the previous list of statements that should appear in a will. The phrase 'give and bequeath' and 'devise and bequeath' has been noted at the start of each clause showing separate intended gift. It can be abbreviated to 'give' so long as your wishes have been made clear.

Example of a will

(A) THIS IS THE LAST WILL AND TESTAMENT OF (B) Edith Mary Baker of Somerset Farm, Non-Such Lane, Burton, Warwickshire made this fifth day of October one thousand nine hundred and ninety-seven.

(C) I hereby revoke all former wills, codicils or other testamentary provisions at any time made by me and declare this to be my last will.

(D) I appoint my husband James Arthur Baker of Somerset Farm, Non-Such Lane, Burton, Warwickshire and my son Richard John Baker of Rose Cottage, Hill Street, Minford, Warwickshire and Mr J Blogham of J Blogham and Sons, High Street, Minford, Warwickshire to be the executors of my will and trustees of my will trust and Mr J Blogham shall be entitled to charge and to be paid for all professional or any other charges for any business or acts done by him in connection with this will.

(E) I express the wish that my body be buried in the graveyard at Burton Church and devise and bequeath the sum of £5,000 to the said church restoration charity appeal.

(F) All gifts are subject to the payment of my just debts, funeral and testamentary expenses and all taxes and duties payable.

(G) I devise and bequeath to my daughter-in-law Mary Anne Baker of Rose Cottage, Hill Street, Minford, Warwickshire my emerald and diamond engagement ring, the oak grandmother clock with brass fixtures standing in the hall of my home, the brooch shaped as an apple with five diamonds.

I devise and bequeath to my grandson Robert Matthew Baker of Rose Cottage, Hill Street, Minford, Warwickshire my stamp collection absolutely.

I devise and bequeath to my granddaughter Amanda Mary Baker of Rose Cottage, Hill Street, Minford, Warwickshire the remainder of my jewellery not previously disposed of.

(H) I give and bequeath half of my half share of the freehold land and property of Somerset Farm, Non-Such Lane, Burton, Warwickshire to my son Richard John Baker of Rose Cottage, Hill Street, Minford, Warwickshire or if this should be sold or otherwise disposed of during my lifetime any other land or property owned by me at the date of my death free and discharged from all sums secured thereon by way of mortgage or otherwise absolutely.

I devise and bequeath to my grandson Robert Matthew Baker and my granddaughter Amanda Mary Baker of Rose Cottage, Hill Street, Minford, Warwickshire the sum of £10,000 each free of tax to be theirs absolutely on attaining the age of eighteen. My Trustees have the following powers:

a. To invest and change investments as freely as if they were themselves beneficially entitled and this power includes the rights to invest in shares and includes investing in property for occupation by a beneficiary.

b. To apply for the benefit of any beneficiary as my Trustees shall think fit the whole or part of any capital or income to which the beneficiary is entitled or may be entitled and becoming absolutely entitled he or she shall bring into account any payments received under this clause.

I devise and bequeath to my sister Mrs Emily Mary Lewis of 22 Mill Lane, Burton, Warwickshire the sum of £5,000, and the picture entitled 'Roses in Bloom' painted by William Lewis and currently hanging in the hall of my house.

(I) I devise and bequeath the residue and remainder of my estate both real and personal to my husband James Arthur Baker of Somerset Farm, Non-Such Lane, Burton, Warwickshire absolutely if he shall survive me by thirty days. If he shall not survive me by thirty days then I devise and bequeath all the residue and remainder of my real and personal estate whatsoever and wheresoever to be divided equally among those of my grandchildren whosoever shall be living at the date of my death.

(J) In witness hereof I have set my hand this day and year first written.

Edith Mary Baker [signature]

Signed by the said testator in the presence of us present at the same time and by us in her presence

Catherine Mary Brown [signature]
High Street,
Burton,
Warwickshire
(Solicitor)

John Henry Willis [signature]
High Street,
Burton,
Warwickshire
(Solicitor)

Notes

1. If you were going to appoint only, say, a firm of solicitors as executors, the first paragraph would have to read:

'I appoint the partners at the date of my death in the firm of Messrs Blogham and Sons of High Street, Minford, Warwickshire [and trustees] to be executors of this my will. The executors and trustees shall be entitled to charge [insert charge if necessary] and be paid out of the residue of my estate all professional and other charges for all business or acts done by them in connection with this my will.'

Do, however, ask any professionals what charges they are likely to make against a current will, as an exact figure for some time in the future could not possibly be given. If it is to be a percentage of the value of the estate, you can insert this figure in the appropriate space as noted above.

2. If your children were to be the sole beneficiaries of your estate, you would need to insert the following clause immediately after the executor's clause (D):

'I devise and bequeath all my real and personal estate whatsoever and wheresoever to my children [name] of [address] and [name] of [address] absolutely if they shall survive me by thirty days.'

You would also need to insert the provision that should your main and sole beneficiaries not survive you by 30 days you would leave your estate to someone else. An example of this would be:

'If they shall not survive me by thirty days I devise and bequeath all my said estate whatsoever and wheresoever to [name] of [address] absolutely or in the event of him [or her] not surviving me for the aforesaid period I direct that my said estate is [insert here what you wish to do with your estate in these circumstances].'

3. In the event that you wish to leave a life interest to your husband, for example, then the following paragraph should be inserted in the will in place of the paragraph after the executor's clause (D). As life interest clauses can cause disharmony because they are restrictive, careful consideration needs to be given before inserting one.

'I devise and bequeath all my real and personal estate whatsoever and wheresoever to my trustees upon trust to sell (to postpone sale) and to invest the proceeds thereof and apply the income for the benefit of my husband [name] of [address] until he dies or remarries whichever is the sooner. Thereafter in the event of his death or remarriage the proceeds are to be divided among such of my children [names] of [addresses] as shall be living at the date of my husband's death or remarriage absolutely.'

As you can see from the sample will, you can make as many and as varied 'dispositions' as you wish, provided that you clearly state that you 'give and bequeath' or 'devise and bequeath' whatever legacy you wish to give and to whom.

Presuming that you wish to make various gifts but that the remainder of your estate is to be divided between your husband and son, in other words neatly cutting the residue of your estate in half, the following clause would need to be inserted at (I).

'I devise and bequeath half of my real and personal estate whatsoever and wheresoever to my husband [name] of [address] absolutely if he shall survive me by thirty days and the other half of my real and personal estate whatsoever and wheresoever to my son [name] of [address] in equal shares absolutely. If either one shall not survive me by thirty days then his share shall accrue to my estate and be given absolutely to the survivor.'

Stating that the residuary estate should go to the grandchildren equally, should the husband and son not survive the stated time, ensures the clean disposal of the estate in case of this eventuality. If you are a widow or widower with a child under the age of 18, you may wish to take this age factor into account and insert the following clause (instead of (F)).

'I devise and bequeath all my real and personal estate whatsoever and wheresoever to my trustees [names and addresses] upon trust to pay my funeral and testamentary expenses and to stand in possession of the residue of my estate and apply the income therefrom for the benefit of my son [name] of [address] until he reaches the age of eighteen and thereafter to him absolutely.'

It would be prudent, in case of a tragedy, to insert the following statement underneath the one noted above in case the minor should also not survive but leave children.

'I devise and bequeath all my real and personal estate whatsoever and wheresoever to my son [name] of [address] and in the event of his death before me for his share to pass to such of his children who shall be living at the time of my death.'

While including the above clauses it is worth remembering when creating a trust for the minor to make allowances should this minor need help with his or her education or living expenses. Indeed, if an accumulation and maintenance trust (see page 115) is established then it is important to allow for income to be drawn within the set rules of the trusts. From 6 April 2010, the trusts are subject to an increase in tax levels from 40 per cent to 50 per cent and can also attract a ten-year charge should the beneficiaries not receive their entitlement at 18 years of age. If no income is drawn and paid across to the minor, then the minor loses the ability to reclaim any tax from his or her payments. Minors, too, have personal tax allowances and if the threshold has not been reached, and provided tax has been deducted and paid, then the difference between this threshold and the level used below it can be reclaimed on the minor's behalf. Payments are sent direct to the minor or parent/ guardian. Without this clause the tax pool is lost when the minor exceeds the age of majority or when the trust ceases.

As you can see in the main will, when leaving a legacy to a relative, it is best that you specify what that relationship is. So, for example, if the person is a half sister, the will should specify this relationship, ie 'to my sister of the half blood'. Always try to give the full and correct names of beneficiaries rather than 'pet' names and always give the last known (or current) address.

If your children are under the age of 18 and you have not already appointed a guardian in the event of your death, then your will can appoint a guardian by the inclusion of a guardianship clause in your will.

When leaving money to charities, note clearly the full name and correct address of that charity, its registration number along with the bequests that you desire to make. Often charities, knowing that you wish to contribute, will supply you with a separate legacy form. It is not, however, advisable to use this unless it is your intention that the charity should benefit absolutely. Instead, include the legacy with the others in your will. When calculating the total value of the estate for inheritance tax purposes, remember to deduct the value of any legacy directed to be given to a registered charity before deducting the inheritance tax threshold and multiplying the difference by the tax rate applicable at the time.

If you are a partner in a business, this fact should be noted in the will and reference made to a partnership agreement, which should have been drawn up on the commencement of that business. This agreement should stipulate the precise division of the firm's shares or your interest. In a two-man partnership, if one partner dies leaving the other half of the business (noted as his property) to his wife, the surviving partner has two options. First, he can agree to buy out the deceased partner's share, or second, he can take his partner's spouse in as a new partner. If the latter instance occurs, a new partnership document must be drawn up. In the case of the former, the surviving partner would have to have sufficient funds available to buy out the wife's share. Of course, the partnership agreement can include contingency plans to ensure that the surviving partner keeps the business afloat.

Lastly, if you wish to leave your body or parts of your body for medical research or for transplant surgery, in addition to carrying a donor card, you can insert the following clause, at (E). Of course, do notify your next of kin of this wish.

'I desire and authorise after my death the use of part [state which] (or parts) of my body for medical research.'

What is a codicil?

When making a simple alteration to your will or when revoking any provision made in it, a codicil can be used. If you wish to change executors or to name a person not previously included as a beneficiary in your will, again a codicil can be used.

By adding this supplement to your will you can include new instructions and delete old ones without having to go through the task of rewriting the whole of the will.

You can make as many codicils as you wish. However, too many might make your affairs complicated and it might be easier and simpler to rewrite your will. As a rule, if any matter is not straightforward, a new will should be written rather than relying on a codicil.

To be valid, a codicil has to be signed by yourself and witnessed (not necessarily by the original witnesses of your will) in exactly the same way as your will. Again, as with your will, these witnesses must not be beneficiaries of your codicil nor must their spouses be named.

A codicil takes the following form:

I [name] of [address] declare this to be a first [or second or third, etc] codicil to my will dated that fifth day of October one thousand nine hundred and ninety-seven.

I revoke the previous bequest to my neighbour Mrs Sally Seward of 22 Highcliffe Road, Weston on Sea of £500 and I in turn give £500 to Mrs Lucy May Smith of 13 Sellwright Road, Weston on Sea.

In all other respects I confirm my will.

This codicil is dated the twenty-second day of January one thousand nine hundred and ninety-nine.
Signed by [testator's signature]

Signed by the said testator in our presence and then by us in his presence

(Here the witnesses sign their names, giving their full addresses and occupations.)

David Smith, High Street, Weston on Sea (Shopkeeper)

Phillip Lewis, Seacliffe, Burton on Sea (Retired Naval Officer)

If you do make a codicil, ensure that you refer to your will, stating the correct date of that will. When obtaining probate, the Registrar will require this document as well as your will and the death certificate.

6

A Question of Tax

In his 1986 Budget the Chancellor officially changed the name of capital transfer tax to inheritance tax. A further but more fundamental change took place in his 1988 Budget with regard to capital taxes in the United Kingdom. From 15 March 1988, whoever lived in the United Kingdom would have their estate – upon death – taxed once assets exceeded £110,000 (current rate for 2009/10 is £325,000; tax year being from 6 April in the previous year to 5 April in the current year). Any monies over that amount would be applicable to a single band of inheritance tax at the rate of 40 per cent. (For family trusts, the rate will increase to 50 per cent from 6 April 2010.)

This change drastically reduced the potential liability that existed before that date on the larger estates. For example, before the 1988 Budget a widow with assets of £700,000 would have paid £326,000 in inheritance tax on her death (see Table 6.1). The example below assumes that she had made no gifts over the past seven years.

	£
House	350,000
Stocks and shares	200,000
Personal effects	100,000
Building society deposits	50,000
Total value of estate	700,000

In tax terminology, gifts are meant as a sum of money or a portion of her estate *given* to anyone before her death. Provided that seven years had elapsed from the time of making a gift until her death, then no tax would be payable on the value of that gift. If death occurred during that period, then a portion of tax would be payable on the value of the gift (see Table 6.2).

Table 6.1 – Prior to 15 March 1988

Cumulative chargeable transfer	Rate of tax	Tax on band	Cumulative tax
0–£90,000	nil	nil	nil
£90,001–£140,000	30%	£15,000	£15,000
£140,001–£200,000	40%	£24,000	£39,000
£200,001–£330,000	50%	£65,000	£104,000
£330,001–£700,000	60%	£222,000	£326,000

Effective rate of tax £326,000/£700,000 × 100 = 46.8 per cent.

Currently any personal gifts made during a person's lifetime in excess of the annual or other specific exemptions, such as gifts on marriage, are known as potentially exempt transfers or PETS for short. These transfers are subject to inheritance tax only if the person who makes the gift dies within a seven-year period from the time of making the gift and their estate falls within inheritance tax.

However, full spousal exemption does not apply if the recipient is not domiciled or deemed domiciled in the UK, unless the donor is the same. If neither are domiciled then only the first £55,000 is exempt. See the section on domicile.

Table 6.2

Years before death	Percentage of death rate (%)
0–3	100
3–4	80
4–5	60
5–6	40
6–7	20

It cannot be stressed too often that sensible tax planning is urged for the growing number of individuals with estates still within reach of the HMRC inheritance tax threshold. For the sake of a few hundred pounds spent now, it could save your estate thousands later. Planning now reduces adverse effects later, whether or not these changes are governmental or from a premature death.

Equalisation of estates

The first basic step for the planning of an estate, assuming you are married or civil partners, is equalisation of the estate between spouses/partners. Each spouse should leave at least the amount of the nil rate band (currently £325,000 for tax year to 5 April 2010) directly to their husband with the remainder to their children, close relatives (other than husband or wife) or indeed to a close friend, assuming, of course, that the estate's value is greater than the threshold. There is a proviso and that is: should this gift be made, would the surviving spouse have sufficient monies with which to live financially? In addition, is the value of the estate worth more than the spousal transfer of the nil rate band on second death? With the answers to the previous questions in mind, if applicable to your circumstances, you should use the amount allowed for the unused nil rate band and not forget to include the home in this division of assets. If the home is a valuable one and represents the majority of your asset holding, then it may be wise to have the deeds altered to tenants-in-common rather than joint tenants. You can then discuss a life interest for your spouse. A solicitor will need to amend the property deeds for you and also to include in both the wills a clause which states clearly whether the estate or your spouse, who holds a life interest, should be responsible for maintenance and repairs. If it is the estate then some capital-generating income would need to be set aside for this. Discussions over whether or not the spouse has to relinquish the life interest if he or she remarries or cohabits will also need to be made clear. The value of the life interest is added onto the surviving spouse's total amount when calculating for IHT, should the will trust have created a discretionary trust not an interest in possession as of April 2006.

From 9 October 2007, the Chancellor announced that any unused portion of the IHT nil rate band from the death of the first spouse/partner could be used to enhance the nil rate band on the second death, provided that no previous tax planning had been done and other criteria had been met. The executor(s) in this instance would have to claim this transfer within two years of the end of the month of the second death. If the first spouse had not used his or her nil rate band, then 100 per cent could be claimed at the rate applicable on the death of the second spouse, eg, if the second spouse died in 2009/10 with the current rate of £325,000, a nil rate band of £650,000 could be claimed.

When claiming this transfer on the second death, proof of the marriage in the form of a marriage or civil partnership certificate has to be sent, along with a copy of probate document of the first deceased and a copy of his or her will, plus any codicils or trusts. A D18 form has to be completed along with IHT216. For married or civil partners, it is now even more important to calculate the value of your estate, and should the combined value of your estate be significantly over the IHT threshold then you still need to consider tax planning methods. Depending on the value in larger estates, the estate may still benefit potentially from the use of trusts and the continued practice of leaving the nil rate band to children and the remainder to the spouse. However, advice from your professional adviser is essential.

Where a valid claim for the transfer of the unused nil rate band is accepted on the death of the second spouse or partner, it results in the calculation seen in Table 6.3.

Table 6.3

Estate on husband's death (02/03) transferred to wife		£300,000
Estate of wife on her death on 5 May 2009		£350,000
		£650,000
Unused transfer from husband's estate £300,000 (100%)		
Wife's estate value	£350,000	£650,000
		Nil IHT to pay

Because of this change, you might be tempted to say 'there is now no need to plan for inheritance tax'. But if you are in the fortunate position of having that amount of assets, effectively you will be writing in your will 'to my children I leave £650,000 and to the Treasury I leave the remainder'. You may feel generously inclined to the tax authorities but 40 per cent still bites deeply into anyone's estate.

Equalisation of assets between spouses not only saves on inheritance tax but, if a future government were ever to introduce an annual wealth tax or decrease the threshold and/or increase the percentage level at which the difference is paid on, equalisation could minimise the effect of this tax as well.

No matter what you decide on, eventually the government will change and the question of capital taxes – limits and/or methods of calculation as has recently happened – will probably be cause for thought once more. The need therefore exists to plan your estate effectively if you think that it will exceed the current tax band and review your plans in accordance with any changes as and when they occur.

'But my estate isn't going to exceed £325,000 or even the unused nil rate band transfer.' When was the last time you valued all your possessions? What is the current value of your house?

Have you recently taken out an addition to your life insurance policy? What about pensions? What savings and investments do you now hold? Leaving aside the possibility of your being a beneficiary of someone else's estate, does your revised calculation now show your estate to be worth over £325,000? Many people revising the value of their assets are pleasantly surprised. 'It won't be any problem, I won't have to pay the tax.' But your estate will and, after all, that estate would have been yours.

Settlements

Instead of using outright gifts to reduce the value of your estate you may instead prefer to use *settlements*. It was the 1986 Finance Act that introduced inheritance tax, which replaced the old capital transfer tax. Under this new Act, gifts made into *accumulation and maintenance settlements* or into *interest in possession trusts* are, as with outright gifts, seen as 'potentially exempt transfers' or PETS, which means there is no inheritance tax liability, *provided* the person making a gift survives a period of seven years after making the settlement.

If you have children, or indeed if you have grandchildren, accumulation and maintenance settlements are suitable. Under this type of settlement the beneficiary will receive income from the trust as a right and by the age of 18 receives the entire holding. After the changes in the Budget 2006, if you wish the age of receipt of capital to be 25 and not 18, then there will be a charge to IHT of 4.2 per cent every 10 years starting from the date of majority, when the 18/25 rule applies, provided that the amount in the trust is over the IHT threshold and the beneficiary is over 18 years.

There are certain rules to follow when considering making this settlement and these are:

1. The beneficiary is entitled to the property of the trust or to an interest in possession on attaining a specified age, which must not exceed 25, see also tax legislation;
2. The income from the trust must either be accumulated within the fund or applied for the benefit of the beneficiary; and

3. Either:
   (a) not more than 25 years has elapsed since the settlement was first made, or
   (b) all the beneficiaries are grandchildren of a common grandparent.

If all income is accumulated with no payment of income to beneficiaries, then reclaiming tax deducted on interest paid cannot be done by the minor and the tax pool for that year(s) will be lost. Remember, children too have a personal allowance.

If the non-executed will/trust document only mentions accumulation and no payment of income for the maintenance of the children, then should you consider the situation requires income, you would be well advised to consult with a solicitor to have this changed for the benefit of the children.

The 2006 Finance Act changed IHT rules relating to certain trusts and resulted in more transactions where trusts had to be reported. Presently these rules are under review with regard to defining the 'value' of the assets in a trust, and whether or not certain assets can be excluded.

Provided that these conditions can be satisfied, all gifts made into the trust are seen as 'potentially exempt transfers' and escape the periodic charge applicable to large *discretionary trusts*. An additional benefit is that there is no inheritance tax charge when the beneficiaries finally inherit all the assets if the rules are met. Of course, once you have made the gift, you cannot benefit or have the gift back or use that gift – in the case of, for example, the gifting of a house, you must pay market rent for your use of it.

There is, as with most things, a minus side. This downside is that if any of the beneficiaries are your own children *under* the age of 18 and receive income from the settlement in excess of £100 per annum, this income is added to your own and you in turn are liable to tax, potentially at the top rate of 40 per cent (50 per cent from 6 April 2010).

The use of *small discretionary settlements* can be most beneficial. These settlements provide a greater degree of flexibility on the distribution of income and capital, provided that the initial amount settled into them is less than the nil inheritance tax rate band. There is no inheritance tax to pay upon setting up the trust and these small discretionary trusts are treated as PETS, and usually escape periodic and exit charges of other discretionary trusts. A *discretionary trust* is one of the few areas of tax planning that does give rise to a lifetime charge[2] if the amount settled exceeds a person's chargeable nil rate band. Even with the death of the beneficiary of a discretionary trust it still does not in itself trigger IHT charged on the fund.

Of all the taxes applied throughout the United Kingdom, inheritance tax is the one which, provided careful planning has been done early enough, can be legally avoided.

Transfers between husband and wife

Transfers between husband and wife given during their lifetime or after death are exempt from both capital gains tax and inheritance tax. However, full exemption does not apply if the person receiving the gift is not domiciled or deemed domiciled in this country, unless the donor is also neither domiciled nor deemed domiciled. In the former instance then only £55,000 is exempt.

Domicile

The understanding of the tax definition of the word 'domicile' is important, although it is a concept of general law and not tax law.

Your domicile is the place which you regard as your permanent home and which you consider to be the country with which you are most clearly connected and, if abroad, can be the place you intend to return to. You can only be domiciled in one place at a time and must positively establish your domicility by setting foot in the country concerned. To make matters more

---

[2] A lifetime charge – as opposed to a death charge – is one that is raised for payment during your lifetime.

complicated there are three different domiciles: domicile of origin, domicile of choice and domicile of dependency.

Domicile of origin usually follows that of your father at the time of your birth, unless your father had died. If this had happened, then you would take on the domicile of your mother. Illegitimate children take the domicile of their mother.

Domicile of choice is the choosing of a new country to live in and to make your new life in – having permanently and *absolutely* abandoned the old country – and having no intention of returning to your old home.

You can have numerous domiciles of choice throughout your life provided that in each case you abandon the old place of domicile with the intention of permanently making your home in the new country of domicile and actually going to live there.

Domicile of dependency means that if you have a child under the age of 16 (or a mentally handicapped child), that child takes on the domicile of the person on whom he or she is dependent. Wives married before 9 December 1974 can choose to adopt domicile of dependency. You are deemed domiciled if you have lived in the United Kingdom after 9 December 1974; for taxation purposes you retain domicile status in the United Kingdom for three years after establishing domicile elsewhere. The tax authorities also deem you 'domiciled' if you have lived in the United Kingdom for most of the past 20 years of tax assessments.

It is important to know whether you are deemed to be domiciled in the United Kingdom for IHT purposes. The taxation officials have certain rules which apply to the definition of the term 'domicile'. They are:

1. You are domiciled here on or after 10 December 1974 and within three years preceding death.
2. You are resident here on or before 10 December 1974 and in not less than 17 years of the previous 20 years.

The Isle of Man and the Channel Islands, for the purpose of IHT, are not part of the United Kingdom, but all other parts, Scotland, Northern Ireland, Wales and England are taxed under the same rules.

Living abroad – residency vs domicile

A considerable number of people have chosen to buy more property abroad and the question of residency and domicile is an important one. The latter entails the purchase of a property overseas, and perhaps other assets, and the changing of your domicile status and living arrangements. But should you retain residency in the UK and be domiciled here also then all property worldwide will be chargeable for IHT.

If you are a resident *and* domiciled in the UK then all your property worldwide is subject to UK IHT and you will also be subject to income tax on any income and in most cases capital gains when you sell, if it is not your main residence. For those individuals who have properly changed their status, ie domiciled abroad and not resident in the UK, then IHT only applies on property situated in the UK. Other taxes due will depend on where the income comes from.

Resident status is the easiest one to change. You must first commence your non-residence status by establishing a permanent residence abroad and not returning to the United Kingdom for a full tax year, ie from 6 April in one year to 5 April in the next year. By leaving, say, in December 2007, this means that your non-residence status only begins after 6 April 2009. Thereafter for each subsequent tax year up to and including the fourth tax year, you must spend no more than 91 days in the United Kingdom as an average. From April 2008, days will count if you are in the UK at midnight. You must count the day you arrive as day one and the day you leave is also counted as a full day if you leave after midnight. If you go over this limit then you must start your residency clock all over again.

Once overseas residency is established then only if you have income generated in the UK, eg a business or investments, will that income be taxed in the United Kingdom at the tax rates applicable.

For the three year rule to be enacted, you would have to be non-resident in the UK for three years with the fourth year beginning and follow in the fourth year the allowed days in the UK. In the fourth year you would be deemed domicile in your new country if certain criteria were met, for example having your own house, joining new clubs and professional bodies and even making plans to be buried in your new country, and also taking into account the visitation rules.

The 17 out of 20 rule is where a person has resided for 17 years out of 20 years in the UK. These rules always take the time as 'actual'. Generally, income tax rules apply for the purpose of determining residence in the UK.

Double taxation agreements do apply to many countries so it is worthwhile checking these out prior to your departure and taking professional advice to see what applies in your instance.

Domicile – future changes

After many years of debate on the subject of domicile, the Chancellor announced measures in his 2008 Budget. Individuals who are not UK domiciled but live and work in this country now have to pay for this 'privilege' with a charge of £30,000 tax, levied for the supposed amount of tax they would have paid in tax on any income from investments had they been UK domiciled. For many, it has left them with a choice: to pay up, to leave the UK and commute back to work (provided they can afford to do this), or to give up their job and UK home and return to their place of domicile.

To change one's domicile is not an easy matter as you are actually born with a domicility and, as previously stated, normally that is considered to be the same domicile as that of your father. For tax purposes in order to change your domicile to one of *domicile of choice* you have to have resided in your new chosen country for a considerable period of time, having proved an intent to live there by purchasing a new home. It also helps to marry a naturalised citizen of that country and to develop business interests there. Arrangements should be made so that your body is buried in that country and indeed that all connections with your former country of domicile be severed, even down to club membership.

Double taxation relief is available if some of the deceased's estate included some foreign property and a foreign tax, similar to inheritance tax, has been paid. Relief can be deducted up to the maximum amount of United Kingdom inheritance tax payable on the same assets. To calculate the amount of relief, you will need to find out the exact equivalent in pounds sterling of the foreign tax paid.

Gifts

Each year everyone is allowed to make an annual gift of money which is tax exempt of £3,000 *per person* against capital gifts. If you do not take advantage of this annual exemption, it remains available to be carried forward, but only for a further 12 months, and only on one occasion. It is therefore important to use this annual exemption each year.

Small gifts

Outright gifts to any one person up to the value of £250 per annum are exempt from tax. This exemption cannot be applied to be used against gifts larger than this amount. You can make an unlimited number of these £250 gifts provided they are to different people and do not exceed this threshold.

Expenditure out of income

This can sometimes be difficult to establish as not only does the transfer have to come out of your normal expenditure but there must also be an element of regularity. In other words, if ever you give it bi-monthly, then this procedure must be kept up. The premiums for a life policy that have been written under trust, for example, but not an annuity purchased on your life, will be treated as a gift for the purpose of inheritance tax, and it can be shown that it falls within the normal expenditure rules as a gift out of income. To qualify under this exemption it has to come out of your 'after tax' income and still leave you with enough money to maintain yourself in your usual standard of living. The gift of the annuity and the policy have to be effected independently of each other. The income portion of the annuity is treated as your income for the purposes of normal expenditure rules, but the capital element is not.

Gifts in consideration of marriage

These are limited to £5,000 if the donor is a parent of one of the marriage partners. The amount reduces to £2,500 if the donor is a grandparent of either of the marriage partners and again reduces to £1,000 if the gift is from anyone else. These gifts must be made *before* the wedding ceremony.

Gifts to charities

There is no limit to the amount of money that can be donated to a registered charity free of tax.

Gifts to political parties

Again, there is no limit to the amount that can be donated to a political party provided that the party has at least two current sitting Members of Parliament or has polled not less than 150,000 votes for its candidates at the last general election.

Gifts for the public's benefit or for national purposes

There is no limit to the amount of money that can be donated, tax free, for these purposes.

By taking advantage of these exemptions, even if there were to be a change in government, gifts that were made at the time of exemptions should prove to be safe from any later changes that might be legislated.

It is worth noting that these exemptions have decreased in relative value as time has passed and no increase or indexation has been allowed.

When is inheritance tax applied?

Inheritance tax, if you are domiciled in the United Kingdom, or deemed to be domiciled, applies at death to all your property wherever it is situated globally once your assets exceed £325,000, current level from 6 April 2009. If you are not domiciled here, then inheritance tax will only apply to your assets which are situated in the United Kingdom over that limit. Assets means property and investments as well as personal effects with a quantifiable value.

Funeral expenses and any debts owed by you at the time of your death are deducted from the value of your estate before calculating the amount of tax payable. The value of any gifts to a registered charity is also deductible. Tax must be paid before probate is granted.

What can be achieved if no prior planning has been done?

Deed of variation

If someone has died and no more than two years have elapsed then their will can effectively be rewritten to take advantage of the £325,000 nil rate inheritance tax band (for 2009/10). This is done by means of a document called 'a deed of family arrangement'. This document is a very valuable tool in inheritance tax planning, but it has to be remembered that:

(a) it can only be made within two years of a person's death;
(b) HMRC must be notified within six months from the date of variation;
(c) the deed of variation cannot be made if any of the legacies under the terms of the will to be covered by the deed have actually been disposed of; and
(d) all beneficiaries must agree to this being done.

Indeed, the prime reason for using a deed of variation (deed of family arrangement) is because the estate in its present form is not tax efficient and a deed is made to make it more tax efficient.

Before having a deed of variation drawn up all the beneficiaries under the will must get together for common purpose and agree to the terms of the will. For example, suppose you die leaving the bulk of your estate to your wife but with the stipulation that upon her death a small portion is to go to one of her cousins. Because she is the sole beneficiary of your will your wife can amend it, with her cousin's consent. You will certainly need the services of a solicitor in drawing up a deed and a tax consultant in planning the most tax-efficient route and putting it to HMRC. After 9 October 2007, the sum of the transfer of the unused nil rate band from your estate and her own – provided she died after 9 October 2007 – could also be used.

The deed of variation takes its name because you are varying the terms of the will. Once a deed of variation has been accepted it is, in effect, taken as the ultimate varied will for tax purposes and treated as if it were the original one.

HMRC has four rules that must be observed before a deed of variation is accepted:

1. A notice in writing must be made by all of the beneficiaries under the terms of the will at the date of death.
2. This written notification must be made within two years after the person's death.
3. The deed of variation must clearly set out the altered parts of the will and the new destination of the property.
4. Written notice must be given to HMRC, otherwise it will not count as a transfer upon death for tax purposes.

Another example of the usefulness of a deed of variation, assuming your estate is over the IHT threshold, is if your estate had gone to your surviving spouse (*note*, no tax is payable upon transfer between husband and wife), then the first £325,000 (provided the spouse also lives in the UK) could be diverted to another member of your family, upon all concerned agreeing to this, and still not incur any inheritance tax. In large estates, a deed of family arrangement could also include gifts to charities, which, as noted previously, are free from inheritance tax.

But suppose you die without making a will? Even if a person has died intestate, provided the main beneficiary, ie the surviving spouse and/or children, agrees, a deed of variation can be entered into.

Before deciding to take this step and going to a solicitor, the main beneficiaries should first consult a tax expert and ascertain how much tax could be saved. If the amount is small, then the fees for rearranging affairs might be as much as the tax payable. But do remember, there is a limited time frame in which to work.

Business property relief

Other tax reliefs that can be used include business property relief. This includes not only a business or part of it but also shares in certain companies. However, it excludes those in property or investment companies. This relief comes in the form of a discount in the value of the assets. The business property relief at 100 per cent has been extended to all holdings of shares in qualifying unquoted companies where death occurred after 6 April 1996 (previously only shareholdings in excess of 25 per cent qualified).

1. A sole proprietor's interest in the business is eligible for 100 per cent relief; a partner's interest also qualifies for 100 per cent relief.
2. Business relief at 100 per cent is also available in respect of controlling interest in a company, including that in an unquoted company (that has been held for two years or more).
3. One hundred per cent business relief is available for shareholdings in qualifying unquoted trading companies. Shares dealt with on the Unlisted Securities Market (USM) are now included as are those in AIM provided they have been held for two or more years.

   In cases where a controlling shareholder transfers assets that were used by the company but owned by the individual only 50 per cent relief is given.

4. For quoted companies valued on a controlling basis, ie a shareholding in excess of 50 per cent, the relief is 50 per cent and that includes land, buildings, machinery or plant.
5. Settled property used in the tenant's business – 100 per cent.

Provided the recipient still owns the property – which must still be in use as a business and as such can genuinely be termed 'business property' – even if the gift falls into tax charge following your death within the seven years, it will still qualify for business property relief.

The recent change in CGT in March 2008 means that Trustees may be able to claim relief on certain business asset disposals, including company shares and security provided that a 'qualifying beneficiary' has a qualifying interest. However, any relief given on Trustees' gains reduces a beneficiary's lifetime relief limit of £1 million. Claims must be made jointly between the Trustees and the qualifying beneficiaries.

On scheme pensions, the Government is closing the loophole which allowed people of 75 years of age or over to be able to pass funds down on their death without those funds being taxed.

Agricultural property relief

In addition to business property relief, where a death occurred after 31 August 1995, there have been improvements made to the 100 per cent agricultural property relief relating to farmland that is subject to an agricultural tenancy that had been transferred with vacant possession following the death of the previous tenant. One hundred per cent relief is also applicable if you have the right to vacant possession and your estate can obtain this in the next 12 months. Importantly, any doubt concerning the transfer of value after Budget Day of 27 November 1995 of qualifying business or agricultural assets made within the seven years before death has been removed. For any other cases the relief is 50 per cent.

For the purpose of woodlands, IHT relief on death charges is available if you have owned the woodland for at least five years or had acquired it via inheritance or gift. However, within two years of the death the inheritor needs to elect to apply for this relief and then no tax implications on the income generated by the sale of the timber on this land will apply. Business property relief can be used provided the woodland was used as a commercial venture.

Relief for succession charges

Where one deceased person leaves assets to another person who themself dies within five years, if the first person's estate has already paid inheritance tax, then should the second person's estate also attract inheritance tax a reduction can be claimed. This is based on the following:

Table 6.4

Period between deaths	% reduction
< 1 year	100
1–2 years	80
2–3 years	60
3–4 years	40
4–5 years	20

To claim this, please ensure that you follow the instructions laid out in the inheritance tax guide with regard to succession charges.

Related property rules

The value of any shares held in a company can be increased because of what is known as the 'related property' rules. Under these rules your holding is combined with another and the appropriate portion of the value of the combined holding is taken against the value for inheritance tax purposes. For example, if you owned 35 per cent of the shares in your family's unquoted trading company and your spouse held another 35 per cent, bringing the total value held by you both to 70 per cent, this would give you full control of the business and much more than a minority holding of a single 35 per cent. What it would mean is that your shares would be valued at 50 per cent of the joint holding of 70 per cent.

Ignoring business property relief, because inheritance tax is payable on death based on the full asset value, in order to plan effectively you should not wait until the family firm has become successful before transferring shares to younger members of the family. Instead, you should transfer the shares to your children before the value increases. The best time to do this is when the company is first formed. The seven year rule on gifts also applies. As with all tax planning measures, agreement should be sought from HMRC before this is done.

Although chargeable transfers have to be reported to HMRC within 12 months of a person's death, interest on late payment of inheritance tax starts to be charged as follows. For deaths occurring between 6 April and 30 September in any year, interest becomes payable from 30 April in the following year. For deaths that have taken place between 1 October and 5 April the following year, interest becomes payable six months after the end of the month in which death occurred; in other words if death happened on 29 October 2008, provided inheritance tax was applicable, interest would be charged from 1 May 2009.

In the 1999 Budget, increased penalties were announced with regard to the late or non-payment of inheritance tax. These are:

1. If those liable for inheritance tax or the dead person's representatives do not submit a full account within 12 months of death to HMRC, a fine of £100 is charged.
2. Giving fraudulent information on this form now incurs a penalty of £3,000 plus extra tax against the personal representative(s). The same penalty applies for giving incorrect information.
3. Incorrect information, ie negligence, by the personal representative attracts a penalty of £1,500.

The tax payable on any land or business assets which Great Uncle Harry may have owned, including controlling shares, may be paid over 10 years.

It sometimes happens that shares are sold within 12 months of a person's death for less than the stated probate value. The person liable to inheritance tax can claim that the sale price be substituted for the original probate value provided that the proceeds are not later reinvested into that same company.

Suppose that you were selling Great Uncle Harry's shares, the probate value being £7,000, and because of a fall in the stock market you have only managed to obtain £5,000; if you are liable to the inheritance tax on his estate, you can claim back the original probate value less the sale price, on the proviso stated above.

A similar rule applies to land. If land is sold for less than the probate value within a three-year period, the sale price can be substituted for the probate price.

Disposing of an asset

If you, as a donor, dispose of an asset to another person but retain an interest in that asset, for inheritance tax purposes it is not seen as being an effective transfer as it has a 'prior reservation'. Under the old capital taxes rules a popular method of tax planning used to be for a couple to give shares in their main residence to their children as tenants-in-common which they then continued to occupy. This transfer substantially reduced the value of the estate. With the introduction of reservation rules it was first thought that this method would be ineffective as the donors would continue to occupy the whole of the house, including the gifted share. However, during the Finance Bill 1986 a government spokesman went on record to state that the reservation rules would not apply in the following circumstances:

> Elderly parents make unconditional gifts of individual shares of their house to their children and the parents and the children continue to occupy the property as the family home, such owner bearing his or her running costs. In

those circumstances it is thought that the donors' occupation is termed as one for full consideration whereby because each has a use of each other's part of the house and each bears the cost of maintenance then the reservation rules can be set aside.

In his March 2004 Budget the Chancellor has brought a halt to homeowners who put their property into trust and continue to live in the house free or pay only a peppercorn rent. From April 2005 these people have to pay an annual income tax charge based upon an assumed real market rent. The tax change applies to schemes already in existence even if they were set up years ago. Home loan schemes or double trust plans appear to have been the Chancellor's main target. Under such schemes the couple sell the property to a trust which gives them the right to live there. The couple do not receive any money for the home, just a promise to pay for the home when the second spouse dies. The debt is then given to a second trust that ensures the children inherit on the second spouse's death. As long as one of them lived for seven years after setting up the scheme then the value of the debt was deducted from the property. However, from April 2005 a higher-rate taxpayer would pay 40 per cent on an assumed market rent, thus negating over the years any IHT benefit. Family wealth trusts will also be charged as of 6 April 2010 as their tax rate increases to 50 per cent.

As trusts can be useful tax-planning vehicles with regard to inheritance tax, it is worthwhile considering the different types of trusts and how effective they can be in inheritance tax planning as well as whether or not it is worth it for your current size of estate. However, if you are going to set up a trust, then you must go to a solicitor and tax consultant and ask for their advice and assistance.

The following pages give a brief description of some useful and more popular trust settlements. Each trust has to be personalised to your own requirements and financial circumstances. Despite the Chancellor's change in trust tax, trusts can still be useful tax-planning vehicles. However, trusts can be costly to run and there is nothing set in stone which means a future Chancellor will not change the tax law governing them and this may affect your trust. Advice should be taken from a specialist tax consultant, who should also ensure competent drafting of the trust and importantly, observe and inform on any changes that would affect it.

Interest in possession trusts

Although not defined in the tax legislation, an 'interest in possession' exists when someone is absolutely entitled to the trust's income. When that interest comes to an end because of the life tenant's death, the assets of the trust are added together with the person's free estate (in other words, whatever is owned outside the life tenancy) to determine the total amount of inheritance tax payable by the tenant's estate. The trustees will become liable to tax on a pro rata share of the total tax payable. If you dispose of your interest during your lifetime, the value of the trust is treated by the tax authorities as a lifetime gift and would be taxed according to the lifetime tax rates applicable to yourself. This means that if your tax rate is 40 per cent, then whatever assets are yours and incur inheritance tax, the gift will also be taxed at 40 per cent.

There are three occasions when no inheritance tax will be payable, and these are:

1. where you have the interest in possession and become absolutely entitled to the assets of the trust;
2. where the property of that trust reverts to the settlor's spouse (the *settlor* is the person who has made the trust out) during the settlement lifetime or, if death occurs, within a two-year period;
3. where the life tenant is the surviving widow or widower of the settlement and the old estate duty (pre-1974) was paid when the spouse died.

The 2008 Finance Bill seeks to clarify IHT rules where interest in possession trusts (IIPs) in existence on or before 21 March 2006 come to an end on or after 22 March 2006 and where these have been replaced with new IIP trusts for the same bene-ficiary. The transitional period for these IIPs has been extended to October 2008. However, it is not yet clear what the provi-sions for the pre-22 March 2006 trusts will be.

Children: accumulation and maintenance settlements

This type of settlement is an extension of a discretionary settle-ment with inheritance tax advantages provided the following criteria can be satisfied:

1. The beneficiaries will become entitled to the trust's assets at the age of 18.
2. The income in the meantime must be accumulated or applied towards the education and maintenance of the child or children.
3. No more than 25 years can elapse since the settlement was first made, and all the beneficiaries are grandchildren of common grandparents. In such a case, provided that bene-ficiaries become entitled to the assets at age 18, there is no tax payable when setting up the trust (assuming the donor survives for the seven years). Inheritance tax becomes due at a 10-year rate of 4.2 per cent from the date of commencement of the trust if the beneficiaries' entitlement exceeds the 18 years of age rule and the assets of the trust are over the IHT threshold; the 18/25 rule then applies.

Previously, if you were a 40 per cent taxpayer and your estate was likely to be well over the inheritance tax threshold, assuming you had grandchildren, it was worthwhile to commence a trust for their benefit. The trust rate of tax stands at 40 per cent, but where sums have been paid out to the child(ren) and where these sums have had tax paid (except of course for tax paid on divi-dends), then the child(ren)'s parents/guardians can reclaim the income tax deducted on behalf of the child or children, assuming that the child(ren)'s personal allowance has not been exceeded.

This is done by writing to HMRC at its repayment centre in Belfast. They will issue a tax reference number in their department for you to correspond, along with a repayment claims form. This needs to be completed and returned to them along with R185 completed by the trust's representative. Following their acceptance of the claim a cheque is then sent to the child.

It is worth noting that if no maintenance payments are made to the children, then any tax pool that exists will cease and not be repaid when the trust ceases.

The trustees need to be aware that on some assets, when they are transferred from the trustees to the beneficiary, CGT may be payable on any gain made, ie property.

Discretionary trusts

With a discretionary settlement no one has an interest in possession as seen by the tax authority and inheritance tax is payable in the following circumstances:

1. When capital is first put into the settlement.
2. When capital is distributed to the beneficiary or beneficiaries.
3. On the tenth anniversary of the settlement, tax is payable on half of the death rate above the nil rate band.

Another type of trust is a two-year discretionary trust as it is a very flexible type of trust and can be used, for example, if you wish your estate to be held in trust for your spouse and/or children for a period of two years from your death. During that time capital from the trust can be paid out to trust members at the executor's/trustee's discretion. It means that your spouse and children can get money when they most need it without incurring a heavy tax burden. The decision as to who needs what and when allows the trust's executor to distribute the estate as tax-efficiently as possible.

Jointly owned property

Property can be owned in two ways. The first is in a joint tenancy and the second is in a tenancy-in-common. In a joint tenancy, when the co-owner dies the surviving co-owner automatically takes over the deceased's half irrespective of provisions in his or her will. Of course, a solicitor should have been used to adjust the property's title deeds to this effect.

Tenancy-in-common means that the deceased's share of the house passes as part of your estate to be distributed under the terms of the will. From a tax point of view, whether the husband inherits his share from his wife or vice versa, if the property is jointly owned by them then the share will be exempt from inheritance tax under the 'surviving spouse' exemption. If the property is owned jointly by two friends or, say, by a mother and son, the share will become liable to inheritance tax.

If a mother wanted her son eventually to inherit her half of the house (held as tenants-in-common), and assuming she is still married, she could write in her will that a life interest goes to her husband but that on his death her son receives her share. By doing this she ensures that her son eventually inherits her half. If, for example, she were a co-owner in a joint tenancy, after her death it would pass automatically to the husband, and if he remarried, his new wife could become entitled to the whole of the house upon the father's death if she were noted as a joint tenant, unless he made a will to the contrary. This could not happen under a tenancy-in-common as the husband and the new wife would live in the house but on the husband's death his first wife's half share in the property would pass to her son.

Inheritance tax wartime compensation payments

Ministers have agreed to extend extra-statutory concessions F20 from 13 March 2002 to include further schemes where compensation to the original victim or spouse for 'personal hurt suffered at the hands of the National Socialist regime during World War II' is paid.

This extended concession treats these payments in the same way as those made to individuals held as prisoners by the Japanese during World War II.

These changes are important as they allow for these compensation payments to be deducted from a person's estate before IHT charges are calculated. Similarly, where one or more amounts are received from any of the recognised funds then it is the total of the amounts received that are excluded from the estate.

As some individuals who had a right of claim may have themselves died, and their spouse becomes entitled to this payment, then it has been stated that '*by concession*, where such a payment has been received *at any time* either by the deceased or by his or her personal representatives under the arrangement', the amount received can be left out of the chargeable value of the estate [italics are the author's own]. It will be interesting to see how the reclaiming of any applicable IHT repayments is received.

More information can be gained by contacting HMRC Capital Taxes Office – IHT at Ferrers House, PO Box 38, Castle Meadow Road, Nottingham NG2 1BB. A helpline for inheritance tax and estate queries is 0845 302 0900.

How is inheritance tax paid?

Inheritance tax forms have evolved over the years and they are now easier to follow and complete than before. The Guides have also been written in a more readable and understandable way. When you contact either the order line (0845 234 1000) or the Capital Taxes Offices, these will be sent out to you on request. Form IHT 200, for example, has IHT 210 as guide notes. Supplementary pages SP1 and SP2, which accompany the supplementary pages, break down the various assets into manageable portions, such as shares, property, pensions, etc. If you have any queries the Helpline will assist you. Forms can also be downloaded from www.hmrc.gov.uk/cto.

If the net estate exceeds the 'excepted estates' limit (£325,000 from 6 August 2009) the executor will be required to obtain a pack from HMRC which will include the IHT 200 and D forms 1–18. When completed, the IHT 200 will be sent to HMRC for tax to be assessed though there is provision for self-assessment. The D18 will accompany the probate application made to the Registry. After making the probate declaration, which is currently an oath, the Registry will hand back the D18, which is then sent to HMRC either showing tax to be paid or noting that tax is not payable. The Registry will issue the Grant of Representation on reviewing the stamped D18 form.

When the executor or administrator has completed the HMRC forms as well as the PA1 form from the Registry, these are received from and returned to the Probate Registry (or in Scotland from the Commissary Office), the Registry will, if it is appropriate, send the forms to the Capital Taxes Office at Ferrers House, PO Box 38, Castle Meadow Road, Nottingham NG2 1BB or to the Belfast office, Level 3, Dorchester House, 52–58 Great Victoria Street, Belfast BT2 7QL. Here the information contained in the forms will be assessed to see whether or not any tax is immediately payable. Tax due on an estate other than a house, property or land or share in a private company must be paid before the grant of probate or letters of administration are issued.

If the assessment is incorrect or you cannot agree with this assessment, you should write immediately to the tax authorities stating the reason why you do not agree with their assessment. Always quote the reference number given on any replies received from the authorities. If dealing with HMRC direct, then you should note all the details of the will; for example, the deceased's name, address, date of death, the date probate was granted and what Probate Registry was dealing with matters and the reference number provided.

As can be imagined, a difficulty arises when the testator has not taken into account the value of the estate grossed up. For example, say you left £365,000 outright and had distributed this same amount under the terms of your will, making no allowance for tax to be deducted from your estate. Your beneficiaries or the residuary beneficiary would only receive a portion of your written declaration because tax would first have to be paid before probate and distribution took place (ie £365,000 – £325,000 = £40,000 × 40% = £16,000, therefore distribution = £349,000). So a word of warning: inheritance tax can damage your wealth!

To make these calculations simpler, HMRC has produced tax tables showing what inheritance tax is due on different amounts of grossed up estates. Once you have valued your estate it may be worthwhile to ask your local HM Inspector of Taxes office to forward a copy to you so that you can make sure that your calculations are correct. (See page 159 for the table on how to calculate inheritance tax.)

Always remember that HMRC works on the principle that the tax payable on the legacy is an integral part of your estate and in most cases must be paid from the estate before distribution can take place.

Any tax that needs to be paid across to the tax authority based on income and therefore income tax needs to be deducted from income and not from capital. Any capital sales may generate capital gains tax payable.

Insurance against inheritance tax

You can 'insure' your estate against inheritance tax by taking out an insurance policy. In order for the proceeds not to be included in your estate, you should have it written in trust for your children, so it will pay out on your death and they can pay the tax against it if necessary. Usually these policies are whole of life ones. However, they also now come under the scope of the 2006 changes because of the 'trust' implications, and care should be taken if following this route. If you consider the insurance policy route, be aware that in committing to a set figure you will have to take into account your current and future asset values against which IHT will become due.

But be warned, it is expensive. Basically, the insurance companies work on the principle that the older you are the higher the premiums become as the day of your 'parting' is that much closer. If you are a smoker then this adds to your cost.

It could be argued that, for the increased premiums asked, if the same amount were put aside and invested wisely then this extra money could achieve much the same end in alleviating the tax burden when it falls, as long as you take into account what you need to earn and set aside for inheritance tax. Of course, the best 'insurance policy' is to make sure that you have already taken all necessary estate planning measures. For large estates and for families then insurance policies are worthwhile tax planning tools.

Most people are pleasantly surprised when working out the valuation of their estate. How to value an estate is explained in Chapter 10. It is important to know what the overall value of your estate is in order to minimise the tax liabilities which your estate or beneficiaries will face. By planning in advance, for example by equalising the estate and the income produced by it, and properly drafting your will, you can ensure that your estate – and your family's affairs – are in a more tax-efficient position.

7

Dealing with Personal Tax Matters after Death

The administrator, shortly after the death of an individual who has died without making a will, has to settle the deceased's personal tax liabilities. He has to see that any income tax, capital gains tax or inheritance tax liabilities are paid to HMRC. Handling these affairs can mean not only paying out money to clear the tax bill but also perhaps applying for a refund of tax from the Inspector of Taxes on R27. Whichever applies, the amounts are seen as either a liability or an asset of the deceased person's estate as at the date of death, and will affect the amount of inheritance tax due.

In April 1996 a new system of tax collection was introduced, known as self-assessment. Over 13 years, we have got used to its rules and regulations. The idea behind this change was that the onus to pay tax falls on the taxpayer (executor or trustee) as it has always done but that the *taxpayer* has to advise HMRC of this liability. Penalties are much higher than before.

As executor, you should be aware that there are a number of time limitations set by the tax authority for raising an assessment for tax on the deceased's estate:

1. Under Section 40(1) Taxes Management Act 1970, HMRC must raise the assessment within three years of the end of the tax year in which the death took place. In other words, if a person died on 1 March 2006, then the assessment must be raised by HMRC no later than 5 April 2009.
2. Under Section 34(1) Taxes Management Act 1970, any assessment raised within the three-year period mentioned in 1 can only relate to the deceased person's six previous taxable years. In other words, if a person died on 6 January 2008 (this would fall within the 2007–08 tax year), HMRC could raise a tax assessment(s) for any (or all) of the previous six years prior to his or her death.
3. If HMRC can show that tax has been lost to the Crown by 'wilful default or fraud', it may raise an assessment on the executor within the previously stated three years relating to any tax year. (A tax year is seen as 12 full months running from 6 April in the first year to 5 April in the following year.) HMRC's assessment starts with the three years and ends within the six years from the date of death.

In the income tax year in which the death took place, the deceased person will be assessed for tax under various schedules right up to the date of death. There is no apportionment of income in income tax law. For example, income from property assessed under income tax schedule A is assessed on rents due to the deceased prior to the date of death regardless of whether the money has been received before or after the date of death. The normal cessation rules apply. In other words, income is assessable to income tax schedule D, cases I to V, and any amounts that are received under the deduction of basic rate tax will only form part of the deceased person's income if the payment date shown falls before the date of death.

For income received after the date of death, the payment becomes income received during the period of administration and therefore there is no question of time apportionment. This makes life somewhat simpler as there is, in general executorship law, the assessment of income tax in the year of death, and this is a relatively simple matter.

Allowable expenses before inheritance tax

The following are the most common deductions made from the gross value of an estate in order to arrive at a figure of net value before the inheritance tax is calculated:

1. certain exempt transfers such as donations to registered charities, political parties with two or more elected MPs, etc;
2. funeral expenses;
3. debts owed at the date of death payable in the UK, although certain gifts after the March 1986 Budget can be disallowed if you made connected gifts to those creditors or the debt was not wholly for your own consideration;
4. legal and professional fees owing up to the date of death;
5. income tax and capital gains tax liabilities up to the time of death whether or not an assessment has been raised at that time.

No allowance against inheritance tax can be made for either probate expenses or executors' expenses. If the deceased had signed an agreement for the sale of a house, for example, but the house was only sold after his or her death, then the agent's fees agreed prior to death but payable on the sale can be deducted for IHT purposes.

Any debts arising outside the UK are normally deducted only from assets that are themselves situated outside the UK.

How does this affect the surviving partner's tax position?

Following the Chancellor's 1999 Budget, both widows and widowers receive a rather raw deal from 6 April 2000. The widow's bereavement allowance has been abolished. This means that a widow who previously would have had a direct reduction in tax no longer gains this allowance – a double blow at a time when the state earnings pension scheme payments for bereaved spouses will be halved. Only the bereavement payment proposed in the Welfare Reform and Pensions Act is allowed but sadly only to those under 60. Fortunately, both sexes will be able to claim it.

Any investment income arising from assets held in the deceased's name after death, ie dividends or interest, will be taxed as if they were owned by the executor. This will, however, not affect the executor's own tax return or his allowance. Once probate is granted and the assets transferred into the survivor's name, then he or she will be taxed on the income earned.

Surviving spouses/partners may receive a greater amount of capital assets on which interest, dividends or rent is paid. This additional income will be added onto the surviving spouse's own tax assessment and may give rise to an increase in tax due if no tax has been deducted at source. In addition, for the surviving spouse/partner over the age of 65, depending on the level of income received, this increase in income may put them over the age-related threshold of £22,900 and he or she could find that they are being taxed with only the benefit of the basic threshold at worst or losing £1 of allowance for each £2 over the threshold at best.

The married couple's allowance was abolished some time ago except where one partner was born before 6 April 1935. If this is the case then the surviving spouse or partner can decide whether or not to use this allowance in the year of death on his or her own tax calculation (assuming he or she has not already done this) or leave it in the deceased's name. The married couple allowance (MCA) is restricted to 10 per cent; see Appendix for allowance.

Self-assessment

From 6 April 1996 a new tax system was phased in, called self-assessment. From this date, it became a legal responsibility of each individual (whether or not in business or employed or retired) to keep full and proper records for both income tax purposes and capital gains. (Of course, individuals should have maintained these records before 1996.) These records must be retained by individuals for 24 months after the end of the tax year in which they relate, 22 months after the end of the tax year in which they relate for executors, and six years and eleven months for business.

The new system removes the onus from HMRC to calculate tax due and firmly places this on the individual or executor. Failure to keep accurate records or late submission of your return and monies due will result in stiff financial penalties.

If individuals or businesses wish to submit their returns and calculations, then these must be with HMRC in paper form by October 2009 and for filing online no later than 31 January 2010 after the end of the tax year or, if later, three months after issue of the return. Late submission of return and late payment incur penalties and interest. A self-assessment of your tax liabilities must also accompany your return. HMRC will do the calculations for you but they must receive all your records by 30 September after the end of the tax year or two months after the date of issue of the return.

As an executor, self-assessment obliges you to keep complete and accurate records and to continue to keep the records of the testator. You will have to complete, as you do now, a return up until the date of death, and one for the period of administration until the day the last of the assets are transferred.

If there is more than one executor of a will or trustee of a trust then each individual is liable to complete a return. In this instance it is best for the executors/trustees to select one of their number, who is familiar with the return, to do this. If no executor or trustee feels able to complete the return, then a tax adviser should be used. Payment for his or her fees is set off against any income that is earned, even if the income is paid direct to the life tenant by the will.

HMRC Nottingham Trust sends out a guide with the Estate Tax Return. It sets out how the calculation is worked out, what expenses are deductible and so on. Trusts for vulnerable beneficiaries may have further relief available.

If returns are late in their submission to HMRC, it has the power to issue a penalty of £100, which itself is interest-bearing; however, if tax due is less than £100 then the penalty will be reduced to equal to the amount of tax due.

Where a settlement under a trust exists, and there is more than one trustee, each trustee will need to make a return and be accountable for errors and omissions in both income tax and capital gains tax.

What is a tax code?

The tax allowance that is given to you is known as a tax code and is shown in the form of figures and a letter. The figures show the amount you are allowed to earn before tax and the letter states which category applies to you. This code is sent to you and to your pension provider or your employer and is based on information that the Revenue receive. If you are in doubt as to its correctness, then telephone your tax office, reiterating your circumstances and details of the income earned and ask for your code to be checked. Likewise, if your circumstances change, then you need to inform HMRC.

Executor's duties

Wherever you live in the United Kingdom, any tax matters mentioned in this book will apply as HMRC – unlike the Probate Registry or Commissary Office – covers the whole of the United Kingdom, except for the Channel Islands and the Isle of Man.

An executor's duties start immediately after a person's death. Often the responsibility for making the funeral arrangements falls on the executor, as does the finance for paying this bill from the deceased's estate. Your duties as executor continue throughout the period of administration, collecting the assets, paying the debtors, which includes any tax due, seeing that specific legacies are paid off and the residuary legatee (the person whom the remainder of the estate goes to) is informed of the balance.

In your final correspondence a letter should be sent to the residuary beneficiary in which you list all the remaining assets available. By doing this the residue is then stated to have been 'ascertained'.

When you consent to the beneficiary taking these assets over it is termed as 'assenting to the residuary bequest'. At the same time as you send this letter you should also send a copy of the estate's accounts and ask the beneficiary to sign them as proof of the formal discharge. When this is done you have effectively ended the period of administration.

It may be that under the terms of the will the deceased created a trust. This will be known as the will trust. At this point you, as the executor, cease to be the executor and become the trustee. It is possible to appoint a new trustee in your place at this time if you do not wish to continue.

Income tax due during the period of administration

From the date of death the executor receives all income which arises from any of the deceased person's estate, some of which will be taxed at source. In other words, the sending organisation will already have deducted tax (unless the deceased account holder was not liable to tax and had signed an appropriate form from the bank or building society). This usually happens with building society or bank accounts; dividends gained from company shares would have had 10 per cent tax (on the gross) deducted at source. Additional tax may have to be paid if the deceased's income was over the relevant threshold. Other income, such as rental from property and so on, is untaxed and is sent directly to the executor and a property account showing gross income less relevant expenditure will need to be done. As executor, it is your legal responsibility to declare all income. This does not mean that your own personal tax affairs are affected.

Although as the executor you are not entitled to claim for a personal allowance on the deceased's behalf, you are entitled to claim for losses made after the person's death while you are running his or her business. As far as the income tax rules are concerned, the death of a trader and the subsequent passing of his or her business to a successor normally marks the end or cessation of a trade.

If you continue to run the deceased's business, then the profits made become liable to income tax under schedule D, case I or II. If you merely sell off trading stock, there would be no income tax liability whatsoever. If the business is either a limited company or a partnership, then an agreement may have been drawn up. Clearly, the terms of this agreement have to be followed. As an executor you may also have to obtain a loan, using the estate as security, so that the inheritance tax bill can be met. It should be noted that the personal representatives of the deceased can obtain income tax relief on interest paid on a loan within a one-year period of raising that loan, provided it was used to pay for inheritance tax. If the interest cannot be relieved wholly in the year when it is paid, it can be carried either back or forward as required. As an executor, you are never assessed to the higher rates of income tax during the period of administration. HMRC can now deduct inheritance tax due directly from the deceased person's bank or building society accounts without the estate seeking a loan, assuming sufficient funds are held in them and upon completion of the appropriate form.

Executors or trustees who live outside the UK should call CNR Nottingham (0115 9742012) for an amended NRL3 form if they wish the rental not to suffer UK tax. When a non-resident landlord dies, any HMRC approval notice to pay rent without tax being deducted, ceases.

Expenses incurred while administering the estate are not allowable for income tax and must be met from taxed income. Interest on non-payment of inheritance tax (which runs from six months after the end of the month in which the death occurred) is also not considered to be an expense and is therefore not allowable to be set against income tax. Executor's expenses are not considered to be tax deductible, including solicitors' charges.

Dividend income received after the date of death forms part of the income of the estate as it was received during the period of administration. This is so even if the accounting year in which it was declared may have fallen before the date of death. All income received during the period of administration is liable to basic rate income tax, which is 20 per cent from 6 April 2008. As from 6 April 2009 the starting band of 10p has been abolished.

The distribution of income to a beneficiary

As an executor you should be aware of the implications of distribution of income to the beneficiary. The amount of income to which a legatee becomes entitled depends on the terms of his or her legacy.

General legacies

A specific sum of money, say £5,000, or an asset, say 'my motor car', is referred to as capital matter. As capital matter it means that the person inheriting it is not entitled to any income during the period of administration unless the will directs that interest is to be paid on the legacy. If this is so, then the beneficiary is liable to income tax under schedule D, case III on the amount received.

Specific legacies

This term refers to a gift of, say, £10,000 of 8 per cent Treasury Stock 2015, and entitles the beneficiary to the interest incurred on a day-to-day basis from the date of death. Any interest received prior to the person's death forms part of the residue of the estate.

Annuities

An annuity may be a gift of, say, £1,000 stipulated in the will to be paid over a specified period of time, say 50 years from the date of death. On each anniversary of that person's death you, as the executor, would have to distribute £1,000 less tax of 20 per cent (or whatever rate of tax is applicable at the time). The beneficiary would receive £800. As it is paid out of income that has already been taxed at the basic rate of tax, the real cost to the estate is only £800.

The residue of the estate

The main beneficiary under the terms of the will is often referred to as the residuary beneficiary and as such is entitled to the remainder of the estate and is also entitled to any income received unless it is left in trust or specified to go to someone else. If this is the case, then the life tenancy of the residue of the estate is only entitled to the income arising after the person's death.

The death of a life tenant does not result in any capital gains tax becoming payable, even if the assets are chargeable ones and have increased in value since the original death.

The tax position in the case of the residue of the estate being given absolutely to the beneficiary is as follows. The residuary income of the estate is the total income *less* the interest and expenses relating to that income. The total income less tax, at the basic rate, and interest and expenses is then grossed up and forms part of the beneficiary's total income. Each year, you would have to supply the beneficiary with a certificate of tax deduction (form R185) which he or she can then use to claim back the deducted tax if applicable.

Where a person has only a life interest in the estate, the tax position is different. The net income for the whole of the administration period, less the interest and expenses, etc, is seen to have accrued evenly over the period and the amount is allocated to each tax year and is grossed up to the basic rate of tax for the year applicable. These rates are:

2009/10 20 per cent
2008/09 20 per cent
2007/08 22 per cent
2006/07 22 per cent
2005/06 22 per cent
2004/05 22 per cent
2003/04 22 per cent
2002/03 22 per cent
2001/02 22 per cent
2000/01 22 per cent
1999/00 22 per cent

Under this rule the amounts may have been taxed on the executor at one rate of basic tax but grossed up on the beneficiary at another rate. Therefore, it would be best, if possible, to distribute the estate within a 12-month period after the date of death and avoid letting proceedings be drawn out for subsequent years.

8

Who Can You Go to for Help?

Some executors would not consider administering an estate without the help of a solicitor. There might be a number of reasons why, such as complexities arising from property within an estate or the existence of a trust. More to the point, however, an executor might not be able to dedicate the number of man-hours necessary to the task of administering an estate. And, of course, personal grief might play an important role when perhaps the executor feels emotionally unable to cope.

If a personal application is to be made but you wish to be excused from acting as executor, you must send a letter to the Probate Registry explaining that you feel you are unable to continue and request that you be discharged from your duties. The Registry will then prepare a formal document known as a *deed of renunciation* for you to sign. This document must also be witnessed. If you are dealing through a solicitor, the renunciation will be prepared for you. Should the will be in your possession, and you wish to renounce your involvement but do not know any relatives or beneficiaries of the will and therefore cannot hand it over to them for their own application, you can hand it over to your nearest Probate Registry along with your renunciation. A formal receipt will be given for the documents and the Registrar's central index will record this should an application be made by a relative or other person.

If you are one of a number of executors or you do not wish to act, you may sign a 'power reserved' form which will be supplied by the Probate Registry. This form effectively says that you do not wish to join in the application being made but reserve your right to make an application in the future if you think it is necessary.

When will you need assistance?

The following is a list of foreseeable complications that might necessitate an inexperienced executor applying for professional advice, whether it is for the entire duty or only part of it:

1. if the deceased owned a business or was a partner in a business;
2. family trusts or life interest;
3. if there are any persons benefiting from the estate who are under the age of 18;
4. loss of will;
5. the possibility of a relative claiming inheritance and possible court action thereafter;
6. an inadequately worded will;
7. insolvency of the estate;
8. if a property that forms part of the estate has an unregistered title;
9. the possibility that unknown debts may arise.

Most of these points are concerned with the distribution of the estate. Before you require help you can start proceedings yourself and speed up the actual obtaining of the grant of probate or letters of administration. This application is a simple matter and then later, if the affairs begin to look complicated, or lack of time or whatever reason prevents you from continuing, you can seek further advice from a financial adviser, tax consultant or solicitor, whichever profession is appropriate to your needs.

Occasionally, situations arise where it is not considered appropriate for you to obtain a grant through the Personal

Applications Department of the Probate Registry. However, it is extremely rare for an application to be refused.

Where do you start?

If in doubt about any matters regarding probate, contact the Personal Applications Department of the Probate Registry and talk to the staff at the nearest Registry to you. They are in the best position to advise whether the application may be accepted or whether it would be best to instruct a solicitor. It should be remembered that even solicitors' applications are eventually sent to the Probate Registry for completion, so the staff there are competent to give you advice on most aspects of the procedures. However, they are not allowed to give actual legal advice outside their field.

Solicitors

If the deceased had been self employed in a partnership or was a director in a limited company, then some form of business agreement may have been drawn up. As the deceased's share forms a part of the estate it is important that you understand the terms of that agreement. At this point, you may seek assistance from the solicitor. Often these agreements include an exit strategy which in turn could include keyman or some other type of insurance. Certainly, a valuation of the business as at the date of death is needed and the business's accountants will need to be involved.

In the case of intestacy, as an administrator you might need a solicitor if complications arise, such as difficulties in tracing missing relatives or living relatives residing overseas. This problem is a fairly common one and solicitors know the many ways to have relatives traced.

Time to update your will

A knock on effect of the credit crunch is that wills written in healthier economic times are going out of date and thousands could be in urgent need of updating.

> Making a will is particularly important if you are not married to your partner but are cohabiting.

With home values plummeting and other investments struggling, many assets in a person's will have lost value. Those wanting to leave friends and family in a secure position after they pass away might find that what they have left in their will has considerably less value than when their solicitor wrote it.

Our recent survey into wills showed that 57 per cent of people do not even know if their will is up to date. It is worth checking it every few years and getting your solicitor to update it where necessary.

Not having a will or a will without provisions for your children could leave them without a suitable guardian. People assume a will is only about monetary value, but what would happen to your children if you pass away?

> DIY wills could prove costly.

The temptation many people have is to write or update their own will. They might only be as cheap as £4.99 to buy, but DIY wills could prove costly in the long run. Drawing up your own will risks exposing your estate to a contested claim after your death and could leave your loved ones with nothing.

A will is the one document that covers absolutely everything that you own and is important to you, so it needs to be watertight, covering all eventualities. Doing it yourself will increase the chances of mistakes creeping in and could even render it invalid.

Many people are unaware of the laws surrounding intestacy, so trying to take on the task of will writing yourself could leave loved ones with nothing, and that could include the house they live in.

> Reducing the tax burden on the assets you wish to leave in your will has an even more relevant benefit for your family and friends in the current economic climate.

Contrary to what many people think, there is no such thing as a common law wife or husband. Under English law, even if a man and woman have lived together for many years and have children, they are not regarded in law as related.

It is essential that anyone with a will who has not looked to update it recently goes to their solicitor to review it.

The Law Society-commissioned research by GfK into wills also highlighted that many young people, those

> 84% of people aged between 25-34 said they did not have an up-to-date will.

aged between 25 and 34, did not have an up to date will (84 per cent).

Many people in that age bracket are likely to have bought a home in the last few years. That is a large asset that should be accounted for in the will, the research, however, would suggest this is not being done.

The research also revealed that 22 per cent of respondents over 65 did not know if they had an up to date will.

That research was carried out in October 2007. It is highly likely that many more people from a range of age groups will not have an up-to-date will following the downturn in the economy.

Making a will should not be seen as a one off process. It is essential to keep updating it whenever your circumstances change and could have an effect on what is left to loved one.

For more information on Making a Will and other guidance on common legal problems, visit the Law Society website at **www.lawsociety.org.uk/choosingandusing/commonlegalproblems.law**

If you need to find a solicitor to help make your will you can visit our website at **www.lawsociety.org.uk/findasolicitor**

> 42 per cent of those widowed, divorced or separated did not know if they had an in-date will.

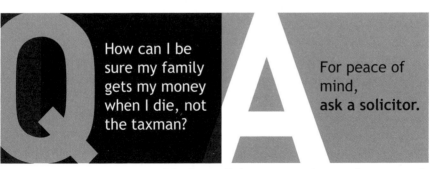

Solicitors will, if you wish, also keep your will on their premises if they have drawn it up for you or if you are a regular client.

Solicitors charge for drawing up a will and this cost can range upwards from £140 per will, depending upon complexities within the estate and the time that has to be spent and where you live. Be aware, however, that some firms of solicitors charge say £140 plus VAT for writing a will when in effect it would have cost them in time spent upward of £180 plus VAT per hour. If they are named as executors, it is worth noting what their charges are, as you may find these could be £200 per hour or more, well in excess of the charge for making the will. If the solicitor does not give you written details of the firm's charge rates within a reasonable time when you first become his or her client, then he or she is in breach of one of the rules of the Law Society's Code of Conduct. Naturally, you have to be realistic when judging how much the bills should be; like everyone else, solicitors have to earn a crust!

The more complicated and lengthy a will is, the higher the charge for the will should be. A word of advice: if your will is likely to be complicated or there are any unusual circumstances, go to a solicitor for help as it will be more cost-effective in the long term. In order to save time and cost, before meeting your solicitor note down in detail your anticipated plans for division of your estate.

Another instance where you could benefit from the professional advice of a solicitor is in the case of intestacy if the estate is valued at over £250,000 where there are children or issue. By current law, the surviving spouse inherits a life interest only in half of the property over that figure of £250,000 and the children receive the other half.

Ambiguity in the meaning or irregularity in the terms of the will may give rise to other instances where professional advice is needed. But again, this need not stop you from initially taking the grant of probate as a personal applicant.

If a person died with debts exceeding assets, despite a will having been made, the estate is insolvent and the beneficiaries would not be able to receive any legacies. In this instance, as executor it would be sensible to employ an accountant to unravel the case, because creditors are paid in a strict order of priority in accordance with bankruptcy laws. The cost of these expenses would be paid for from the estate even before any beneficiary or creditor. This particular problem can throw out complications which are many and varied, one being that claims submitted may exceed the known sum owed.

Another complication can be the possibility of someone making a claim against the estate, seeking to gain a share or a larger share or money that the deceased owed or money supposed to be owed to the deceased. Advice from your solicitor would be essential since either negotiations will need to take place to decide on the portion to be awarded (if the claimant does have a case) or because the claimant contesting the matter is taking the case to court.

These may all sound quite alarming but in the majority of cases matters are relatively straightforward with complexities rarely arising. Simple problems can be dealt with by asking the staff at the Personal Applications Department at the Probate Registry what the best course of action would be or whom you should go to. You can seek advice from professionals other than solicitors or accountants with regard to wills, trusts and tax planning. Do ensure that you thoroughly check the advice given with your solicitor or accountant, who should not have a vested interest.

The Law Society

The Law Society is the public's watchdog for their solicitor members' actions. They also act for their members, the solicitors. Therefore, should you feel that a solicitor has overcharged you or has been negligent, the Law Society – once presented with your complaint and proof – can investigate on your behalf.

Book Aid
International
www.bookaid.org

Books change lives

Poverty and illiteracy go hand in hand. In all the countries where we work, more than half the population earns less than a dollar a day – making books a luxury few can afford. Many children leave school functionally illiterate, and adults often fall back into illiteracy in adulthood due to a lack of available reading material.

Book Aid International knows that books change lives

Books can bring hope to some of the poorest readers in the world, giving people of all ages the chance to make opportunities for themselves. Books are urgently needed in sub-Saharan Africa, where 151 million people remain functionally illiterate.

Every year we send over half a million books to our partners in 12 countries in sub-Saharan Africa, to stock libraries in schools, refugee camps, prisons, universities and communities. Literally millions of readers have access to books and information that could teach them new skills – from keeping chickens to getting a degree in Business Studies or learning how to protect against HIV/AIDS. Many more will know the pleasure of losing themselves in a novel.

"In simple words, I would say that books have changed my life. Now I know myself much better than before. I know where I come from, where I am and where I am going."

- Juma Haji Juma, Zanzibar

Our supporters make it possible for us to continue our work. Each donation or legacy that we receive has the potential to make a long-lasting impact on education for hundreds, if not thousands of readers. Please do contact us on 020 7733 3577 for further information, or go to our website at www.bookaid.org.

Charity No. 313869 Company No. 880754

39-41 Coldharbour Lane, Camberwell, London SE5 9NR

T + (0)20 7733 3577   F + (0)20 7978 8006
E info@bookaid.org   www.bookaid.org

Book Aid International is a charity and a limited company registered in England and Wales.

advertisement feature

Give a little *extra* to help a disabled child and their family.

Bringing up a severely disabled child is extremely difficult. A family's physical, emotional and financial resource can drain away very quickly. It costs three times as much to bring up a child with a disability.

Everyday things like new clothes or school outings become unaffordable luxuries and many disabled children's families are more likely to live in poverty and debt.

That is why families value the support from the Family Fund so highly. We have helped families with disabled children since 1973 with grants for things that make life easier and more enjoyable for the disabled child, young person and their family, such as washing machines, driving lessons, computers and holidays.

Most of our funding comes from government and as such has strings attached. We can only help with grants for severely disabled children under 18, whose family live on a very low income.

Often we are unable to help at times when a family needs us. If a child dies, our support must end.

Family Fund *extra*

That's why last year we set up *Family Fund extra* to offer support to all families with a disabled child whatever their situation. So when the Cook family couldn't afford to buy a headstone for their young son, *Family Fund extra* covered the cost. When the Murray family couldn't pay their heating bill one cold winter, *extra* stepped in.

Family Fund extra gets no government funding. It depends on the generosity of individuals. With your help, we can continue to provide invaluable support to even more families.

To help us help disabled children, please make a donation or leave a legacy in your will. Give a little …help a lot!

Every penny you give will go to families with disabled children. That's £1 in every £1 going to help make a difference to the life of a child or young person with a severe disability

To make a donation or leave a legacy to **Family Fund *extra***, please call 01904 550007 or email epp@familyfund.org.uk

family fund
helping disabled children

Family Fund extra is a trading name of Family Fund Trading Limited, a company registered in England (number 0629312) which is a wholly owned subsidiary of The Family Fund Trust f Families with Severely Disabled Children, a company limited guarantee (number 03166627) and a charity (number 10538 registered in England. Registered Office: Unit 4 Alpha Court Monks Cross Drive, Huntington, York, YO32 9WN.

The Law Society now sells a document called a 'Personal Assets Log', which can be used to list the location of all your important papers, whether they are your will or the deed to your property. Whether or not you decide to use the log, it is a good idea to make known to your immediate family the location of all relevant documents.

The Probate Registry

The Probate Registry is part of the Family Division within the High Court structure and as such comes within the Civil Court responsible to the Lord Chancellor's office. The Registry dates back to Norman times when Bishops' Courts began to administer the wills of the deceased.

In 1357 the Courts were required by statute to pass on the administration of property from the Bishops' Courts to the deceased's closest relative. In 1858 a further change took place when the District Probate Registries were introduced as a division within the Probate, Admiralty and Divorce Division of the High Court. In 1970 the Administration of Justice Act placed the probate section in the newly founded Family Division within the High Court, where it remains today.

The Probate Registry in England and Wales is unusual in that it provides people with advice and assistance that may be needed in order for them, as individuals, to obtain the grant of probate or letters of administration. In Scotland, the Commissary Court does give assistance but this is limited to small estates.

Changes to the Probate Registry

Far-reaching changes were proposed for the Probate Registry, and a consultancy exercise carried out. In the proposal the current Registries and Sub-Registries were to be closed, leaving some six or so Probate Registries nationwide. To this end an amalgamation of telephone numbers/helpline numbers between the Capital Taxes Office and Probate is already in place and working. However, the call centre staff are only trained to deal with standard queries, and if it does not fall into this category your call will have to be transferred to another office. Happily, these proposals to reduce the number of offices have been abandoned and the nationwide network is to remain for the time being. Other positive proposals, such as a joint helpline, will also remain.

Under the present system, before probate is granted appointments have to be made to swear the accuracy of the submission. Under the proposed changes there will be no appointments, and the documents submitted will be signed for as true and accurate by the executor. The oath will be replaced by a statement of truth.

How can it help?

The Probate Registry is the linchpin of the proceedings. Its equivalent in Scotland is the Commissary Office.

The main function of the Registry is to give a grant of representation to the executor or next of kin. This grant is a document bearing the court seal, which states that the person named is authorised to deal with the estate. In fact, the document empowers that person to do anything that the deceased could have done if he or she were alive.

The Registry cannot advise you on making a will. It can, however, deal with any queries you may have in connection with proving the will.

Probate Registries and Probate Sub-Registries are open daily during normal office hours. The probate administration system in England and Wales is a three-tiered one. Currently, there are 12 District Probate Registries and, of course, there is also the Principal Registry of the Family Division at First Avenue House, High Holborn, London. The Registries also have Sub-Registries linked to them. There are also small Probate Offices which deal only with personal callers. These offices may be open for only one day a week or, in some cases, one day a month. Local Probate Offices are linked not only to Registries but to Sub-Registries as well. You will be asked which office is most convenient for you to attend. For a list of Probate Registries and their local Probate Offices, see Appendix 4.

All branches send out application forms, which start the whole proceedings, from their Personal Applications Department. Proceedings are straightforward.

Upon telephoning or writing to the Registry you will receive an envelope containing all the forms that are needed. The turn-round time for dealing with these is usually two or three weeks, although proceedings can be speeded up. The delay is not caused here but usually when the executor is trying to pull together all the details of the estate.

A probate fee is payable for estates over £5,000 at a flat rate of £90 for deaths after 26 April 1999. No fee is charged for estates under £5,000.

Once probate has been granted, executors can proceed to collect in and transfer monies to debtors and beneficiaries.

When neither a will nor a relative can be found the probate Treasury Solicitor will take over these duties. The Treasury Solicitor will also make enquiries on behalf of the Crown to trace relatives. After considerable checking to see whether there are any living relatives with valid claims, if none can be found then he or she will declare this fact. Only then does the Crown become entitled to the estate. (It is possible that a dependant of the deceased may make a claim against the estate; for example, a common-law husband or wife, or close friends who helped the deceased over the years without payment, or creditors.)

There are three types of document issued by the Probate Registry, namely Grant of Probate when there is a valid will with executors applying; Letters of Administration (with will) when there is a valid will but executors have not been appointed or for some reason are not applying; or Letters of Administration given when there is no will. These are collectively known as Grants of Representation.

There are three areas where Grant of Probate or Letters of Administration may not be needed:

1. If the property consists of cash (ie physical notes and coins), if the effects are household ones or a car, and provided there is no dispute between the immediate relatives as to the distribution.
2. If there is no more than £5,000 held in savings accounts or in National Savings and pension funds, it is possible that the sums may be released without the need for a grant. However, this is discretionary and the National Savings Bank may ask for a grant to be taken if it considers that circumstances require it.
3. Individual sums of money in banks and building societies do not exceed £5,000. However, many of the banks make a charge for preparing documents.

Where else can advice be sought?

The time to get in touch with your tax consultant should be before you start to make your will but as an executor after the death you may be faced with tax implications on which you need advice. Like the solicitor, the consultant will charge a fee for his or her time. But remember, not all accountants have estate planning experience and you need to check carefully that your chosen consultant does. Here again, ask how much the consultant charges per hour.

Your bank will also be able to offer help. Banks too charge a fee for dealing with probate matters and that charge can be steep, up to 5 per cent of the estate's value plus a withdrawal fee as well. Banks and solicitors also keep your will for safe-keeping, or you may file it at your local Probate Registry or at First Avenue House. Some banks and solicitors charge an annual fee for storage of your will. The Registry's fee is £15 and is a one-off charge.

If it is necessary to have a bank account for the estate (known as an *executorship account*), remember to ask the bank what charge will be levied. Usually a bank charges a fee for administration – deducted from the account. But because of increased competition not only between banks but between building societies as well, charges and services are constantly changing. With some building societies now offering a banking service, it would be worthwhile shopping around for free banking.

Another organisation that can help is the Citizens' Advice Bureaux. This organisation has the advantage of having offices in all the major towns and cities throughout the United Kingdom. If one centre does not have the information, it can refer to a larger centre or recommend whom to go to.

When valuing the estate you may need to obtain valuations from different sources, depending on the estate's assets and, more importantly, the value in the estate. (If the estate is well under the inheritance tax threshold, then estimates from property valuers or jewellers will not be necessary.) For example, you may need to approach estate agents for property valuation or indeed to sell a property, auctioneers for furniture and jewellery and so on. Do ask what the valuation will cost. In addition to these 'property' valuations you will have to write to organisations such as banks and insurance companies, asking for a valuation of accounts held or insurance policies. You might have to write to a publisher to ask for the current amount due on the royalties from a book; the list of contacts goes on, depending on the nature of the estate's assets. All valuations must be as at the date of death.

9

Documentation

Death certificate

One of the first duties of an executor may be to register the death and collect the death certificate. When doing this at the Registry for Births, Deaths and Marriages, Form PA2, entitled *How to obtain probate*, may be given to you. Basically, the booklet tells you how to proceed with probate, who can apply for the grant and where to apply.

The simplest way of receiving all the relevant forms is to telephone your nearest Probate Registry (or Sub-Registry) and ask for the forms to be sent to you, or download Form PA1 from the Probate Registrar's website on www.courtservice.gov.uk. (For a full list of Probate offices see Appendix 4.) The forms you will receive include not only the probate form but also tax declaration forms which will eventually be sent off to the Capital Taxes Office.

Depending upon the circumstances of the death, an initial medical death certificate is usually issued by the hospital authorities or the general practitioner in attendance where death occurs at home. In the case of sudden death, this is only issued once the autopsy has been carried out. The certificate, given to the closest relative or known executor, has to be sent or taken to the Registrar of Births, Deaths and Marriages within five days of the date of death. That Registrar will then issue the formal death certificate.

It is advisable to purchase extra copies of the death certificate at that time, as you will need to send a copy to each company where assets are held. If you have obtained only two copies, you will have to wait for these to be returned before sending off your next letter, thus delaying the procedure. Ask for these copies to be returned to you. The same advice to obtain multiple copies of probate will prove useful and cheaper.

It is unfortunate, but there are occasions when death occurs while abroad, causing added strain on the next of kin. The first thing to do is to register the death with the appropriate authority in the country where the death occurred. An autopsy may be needed before a death certificate can be obtained. The British embassy or consulate in that country can help with these arrangements and in bringing the body or ashes back to the United Kingdom; you can also register the death with them.

Unless you are insured for such eventualities, the cost of bringing the body back to this country has to be borne by the estate and the cost can be high. Of course, these costs will eventually be deducted from the estate as a debt. The embassy or consulate can help with a small interim loan to facilitate this wish but it will only cover a tiny portion of the overall cost.

What is a grant and why is it necessary?

A grant is in effect a court order. It is your legal proof of title to deal with the estate. Without it some companies and banks will not release money or assets held in the deceased's name. The grant gives authority for these assets to be passed on to the named person to deal with.

As a simple rule of thumb you may certainly need a grant if the property is solely owned by the deceased in his or her name or if the estate exceeds £5,000.

After contacting the Probate Registry you will receive a number of forms, including Form PA1 and IHT205. These must be completed and returned to the Registry dealing with the application by all personal applicants. The following section explains what these are.

What are all these forms for?

Once you have advised the Personal Applications Department at your local Probate Registry, the following booklets and forms will be sent out: PA2, PA1, IHT206, IHT206A and IHT205. IHT200 and booklet IHT210 may also be sent.

Form IHT205 is the basic inheritance tax form for estates below the excepted estates threshold. This threshold now shadows the IHT threshold. If the estate is over this limit then a telephone call to the Capital Taxes Office (CTO) will ensure that the full IHT pack is sent to you. This pack contains IHT200 along with its notes entitled IHT210. In addition, there is SP1, which contains schedules D1–D18 and SP2 booklet. Not all these schedules will need completing as the schedules are specific to certain holdings, such as property or shares which the estate you are dealing with may not own. However, D18 has to be completed as without this being authorised by the CTO, probate will not be granted.

At first, IHT200 appears daunting but its guidance booklet IHT210 is well-written and, for the subject matter, easier to follow compared to previous Inland Revenue documents. If you are unsure as to the precise meaning of a particular term or have a general query, contact the information office of the CTO and they will assist.

For estates over £325,000 in gross value, where the part of or whole of the estate is not passing to surviving spouses, civil partners or registered charities, then IHT200 will need to be completed. When claiming the unused nil rate for a deceased spouse, then the death certificate for the first deceased and probate certificate, and marriage certificate will also have to be sent. If the value is at the excepted estate threshold or more and part or all passes to a surviving spouse, civil partner or registered charity, then the form IHT205 needs to be completed.

IHT200 must be sent in within 12 months after death and if this has not been done in that time and without a reasonable excuse then a penalty of £200 may be charged. Should the delay continue to two years after death then there can be an additional penalty of £3,000 charged. Interest is charged on any outstanding IHT due.

For Scotland, instead of completing PA1, form C1 needs to be completed for all estates. Form IHT200 needs to be completed in Scotland for all estates plus supplementary relevant pages except where Box 14 on page 1 is completed to say that the deceased was domiciled abroad or that the deceased was only treated as domicile for assets held and the grant is needed for land as a settled property.

If in doubt, speak to your local Capital Taxes Office (the national helpline number is 08453 020 900) or visit the website at www.hmrc.gov.uk/cto.

Details of the forms sent out by the Commissary Office in Scotland or by the Capital Taxes Office are to be found in Chapter 11.

What happens next?

Once these forms have been completed they should be returned along with the death certificate and original will to the Personal Applications Department of the Probate Registry along with the codicil(s) if such exist. It is advisable to keep a photocopy of each form for your records.

Once the staff at the Probate Registry have had a chance to look at these forms you will be invited to attend a meeting at the nearest office to confirm the accuracy of the information supplied. Usually only one visit is necessary. It is at this visit that you will be asked to swear to the correctness of the form or, when the new rules are introduced, make a statement of truth. Any small changes can be given at this time. Once this is over and any fee and tax due have been paid, you will be given an approximate timetable for when a grant of probate will be issued. A grant of probate will not be issued if there is any inheritance tax owing or if the grant of probate fee has not been paid. The responsibility of the Probate Registry ends when the grant is issued.

Of course, depending upon the complexities of the estate the time taken to complete these forms will vary. You may find a considerable amount of time has elapsed between you asking for the forms and returning them as in the meantime you have had to assess the estate and value its assets.

A grant will not be issued if there is any objection registered in respect of the estate and will only be actioned once it has been resolved. If the objections cannot be resolved, then in all probability the matter will be referred to a judge in the Chancery Division of the courts. However, before that, the objection may be heard at the District Probate Registry to ascertain if there are any valid points.

Again, if you have any doubts about whether or not your application is suitable for a personal application, speak to the Probate Registry staff.

10

Valuing and Administering the Estate

The example of a will shown on pages 84–87 will be referred to in this chapter to take you, as an executor, through the different jobs that have to be done when valuing an estate and administering a will. The only variation to this will, of course, is that you are seen as the executor.

As an executor you will know where Edith's will is located; also general instructions, such as her wish to be buried in the local church's graveyard. Edith's estate is valued at £380,610 after expenses, and after stated bequests the residue or remainder has been left to her husband, James. There is no mortgage on the farm and although the current (April 2009) threshold of inheritance tax has been breached, no tax is due as the estate's residue was left to her husband. Once this has been done and all debts settled, the half share of the farm can be conveyed to Richard, her son. Any running costs incurred during this time can be settled by the estate; see Chapter 7 for tax considerations. As a rule of thumb, however, remember that tax is payable by the individual beneficiary (unless stated to the contrary in the will) in direct proportion to the value of the gift which is in relation to the total taxable estate.

The same principle applies to a loan secured against an asset that forms part of the estate. For example, should Edith have taken out an overdraft before her death with her portfolio of shares as security against the loan, when Richard inherited the shares he would have to settle the overdraft unless Edith had stated in her will that the overdraft was to be repaid by the remainder of her estate. If Edith had left half of the portfolio to Richard and the other half to James, both would have to settle the debt in direct proportion to the value of their individual inheritance. Moreover, if Edith had intended to give the assets freely without any liability, unless she made those wishes clear in her will, her beneficiaries would have to repay any debts secured against the gifts noted in the will.

If Edith had given a loan to another person and that loan had not been repaid or not repaid in full, then the amount left has to be added to the estate's value. Any interest paid should have been declared to HMRC on tax returns covering the period of the loan. Penalties and interest are charged if this has not been done.

It is best to obtain a number of copies of a death certificate from the Births, Deaths and Marriages Registrar as it is cheaper to obtain them there rather than at a later date. As executor you will have a rough idea of how many certificates are required as a copy should be sent to each organisation holding Edith's assets but asking them to return the copy when its use is finished.

Armed with these copies, you can now send letters to Edith's bank, building society, National Savings, indeed all organisations involved. In the letter you must explain that you are the executor and that you are in the process of applying for a grant of probate. Proof of the death in the form of the death certificate should be enclosed. Request a statement of account, including interest if applicable, up to the date of death and the tax year if it has passed recently. Although not necessary if joint accounts are held, if Edith had been a single person you would have to ask the bank or building society to freeze the debits and credits going into and out of her accounts. All queries would be forwarded to you.

Another incidental job often overlooked is the redirection of post. You should arrange for a redirection of Edith's post and as the precise length of time of your executorial duties is not known, it is best to arrange redirection for 12 months.

Notification of her death needs to be advertised in the local paper. This action ensures that any person with a claim against her estate can come forward.

How to start

Before the forms arrive you should start to make a list of all Edith's assets based on information to hand and also that information noted in her will. Do not write on the original will. Against each item you note its value if known. For some of these assets this may prove difficult and so help should be sought from the appropriate source. For example, Edith had a sizeable stamp collection. Stamps are notoriously difficult to value and expert advice should be sought from a philately society or by approaching an organisation, such as Stanley Gibbons, which deals in stamps. Written valuations should always be asked for. Bank statements will have arrived showing account values as at the date of death.

With these valuations to hand you can now start to prepare a more detailed inventory of Edith's estate.

As part of your duties, you would also have to inform utility companies and the local authority regarding council tax. If a pension were being received then the pension provider(s) would also need a copy of the death certificate informing of Edith's demise.

Property

Although not essential, it is important to get a professional valuation on property unless you are able, on the basis of other properties nearby and recently sold, to make your own valuation. HMRC may, after the grant has been issued, decide to send round its own official, the District Valuer. He or she will value the property based on his or her own opinion of the current market price for that type of property in the area, which might differ from that considered by the estate agent/surveyor to be realistic. If you do a valuation through an estate agent, you can put the lower of the two prices down. If the District Valuer thinks that it is too low, he or she can amend it upward, but should you put the higher of the two values down you are stuck with it as chances are that he or she will not reduce the amount. It is advisable in the current market conditions that professional property values are sought.

Council tax was introduced in April 1993. Wales has already had its values revised. The current tax was based on property prices which were seen as the ones prevailing two years before 1993. Since then, there has been an increase in the market price of houses in most areas followed by a drop of some 17 per cent. Naturally, this has led to debate on property valuations and the tax subsequently charged. If in doubt, the best course of action would be to seek professional advice from surveyors, your solicitor or your local Council.

The District Valuer does not have time to come round and inspect all properties that form part of estates. But he or she will almost certainly do so if a clearly inaccurate low valuation is given.

If a house is to be sold, your own estimate will serve instead of one from an estate agent. This is because the actual value of the realised price will have to be notified to HMRC after the sale.

In Edith's case the farm was owned with her husband as tenants-in-common, and in the directions laid out in her will her share passes on her death to her son. However, for inheritance tax purposes her share still has to be valued. It is worth noting here that should Edith have left her half share to her husband, then such a transfer between husband and wife would have been exempt for inheritance tax purposes.

Let us say that the farm was valued at £570,000; Edith's half share would be £285,000. Should there have been a mortgage, then her half share of this would have to be deducted from the value of her half of the house. So, say the mortgage was £40,000, Edith's liability under the mortgage would have been £20,000, making £265,000 of equitable value. Whoever held the mortgage to the property would have to be informed and an exact figure requested as to the outstanding mortgage at the date of death. That sum would have to be paid either by her estate or the person the property was left to.

By value, the tax authority means the price that the property could be sold for if it were put on the open market with *vacant possession* on the day that Edith died. If the house were tenanted, then a lower value is given to take account of this restriction provided the tenancy did not occur after death.

If you were not sure whether the property was held jointly, an examination of the title deeds would be necessary.

The first valuation hurdle is over. Edith's estate is clearly solvent, with her assets exceeding any liabilities. All legacies can therefore be met in full.

Now you would have to enquire whether Edith was a beneficiary of a trust or life interest from any of her ancestors or other persons' estates. If she had been, then exact details of the inheritance would have to be obtained. For this example, Edith was not a beneficiary of a trust or life interest.

HMRC requires the precise value of items from pensions, life and endowment policies to building society accounts. But if it is clear that the estate is a small one, then approximate valuations are accepted by the Probate Registry.

Based on the response from each organisation that you have written to, once probate has been granted, a copy of the official grant should be sent to each company for their records. All copy letters either sent to you or received by you should be kept on file.

Example 1. Inventory and valuation of Edith Baker's estate

Details	Approximate value £
Somerset Farm (value £570,000; half share £285,000)	285,000
Jewellery: diamond and emerald brooch	1,650

engagement ring and wedding ring	800
other jewellery	2,800
Antiques:	
grandmother clock	3,600
chaise longue	1,500
four-poster bed	2,500
2 Victorian button-back chairs	850
1 painting, early 19th century	2,500
Investments:	
National Savings certificates	8,000
Building society account (1)	5,000
(account no 0000000)	
Building society account (2)	2,500
(account no 1111111)	
Premium Bonds	500
stocks and shares (see separate list)	15,000
stamp collection	6,800
Insurance:	
endowment policy (no 000002)	15,500
(with profits, to be verified)	
life insurance policy (no 000332)	25,000
Other miscellaneous items	5,450
Total of estate	384,950

Debts	£	
Funeral expenses	2,250	
Miscellaneous debts before death	2,000	
Total liabilities	4,250	

Probate fee	90	4,340
		380,610

Inheritance tax, nil as transfer between husband and wife.

Example 2. How to calculate inheritance tax on A. N. Other's estate

(Note: this does not relate to Example 1.)

		£
Total value of estate, say		350,000
Less		
Funeral expenses	2,250	
Half share of mortgage	20,000	
	22,250	327,750
Less current allowable level of inheritance tax		325,000
		2,750
IHT payable		2,750 × 40%
		1,100

The following is a sample letter that should be sent out to each organisation holding estate assets.

Example 3. Letter requesting details on the estate's behalf

---

12 Calthorpe Lane,
Bearwood,
Warwickshire BR2 2PJ

16th June 2009

The Manager
Birmingham Building Society
2B High Street
Birmingham B2 2RT

Dear Sir

I am the executor of the will of the late Edith Mary Baker of Somerset Farm, Non-Such Lane, Burton, Warwickshire who died on the 26th day of April 2008. I am writing to request the following information as to the exact value of Mrs Baker's assets held in her name with your organisation at the date of her death. If there are any details missing please supply them.

Account number: XP12345
Type of account: Savings
Date account opened: 29 March 1999
Value of account at date of death:
Interest accrued up to date of death:
Interest accrued since death up to the date of letter:
Has tax been deducted up to date of death?
    If so, what amount of tax?

If you hold any other accounts in Mrs Baker's name then please advise.

Please supply Tax Deduction certificates to tax year end.

I enclose a copy of Edith Baker's death certificate. Please take a copy and return the original to me.

Probate is being applied for and I will write to you again once I have received the Grant of Probate.

Would you please notify me of any formalities needed before you release the money to me.

Yours faithfully,

J G Person

National Savings certificates

As Edith had bought National Savings certificates you would need to obtain a claims form from your local post office. This is then filled in and sent to the address printed on the back of the leaflet. Each certificate number has to be noted on the form with its individual value and number of units. Also needed is the certificate's serial number and the date of issue. This action would also apply should Pensioners' Bonds be held.

Premium Bonds

When assessing Edith's Premium Bonds, if you are uncertain whether you have got all the certificates you should write in the first instance to National Savings, Government Buildings, Marton, Blackpool FY3 9YP or telephone for further information 0845 964 5000. This address also applies if seeking information on income bonds or other National Savings Investments and the same telephone number also applies for any National Savings Bank accounts. As with all letters that you write, do quote references noted in previous correspondence. Remember to keep a copy of any letters and documents received or sent.

As Premium Bonds have a face value with no interest being paid, they do not need an official valuation, merely the number held totalled up.

Premium Bonds cannot be transferred to beneficiaries. The same is true for National Savings. Nor will the Bonds and Stock Office pay out any money to the estate without receiving the grant of probate. National Savings can transfer ownership of their various products upon receipt of proof of grant of probate, assuming the sum is £15,000 or over and the original certificate is sent in. If the sum is less than this and if the grant has not yet been taken out, then upon sight of the death certificate and a copy of the will the accounts can be transferred.

It is best to leave the Premium Bonds *in situ* until the final stage, just before distribution. But you must advise the Bonds and Stock Office of your address and your role as executor. Should a bond win within one year of the death, the cheque can be sent to you on behalf of the estate once probate has been granted. The money received goes directly into the executorship account for the beneficiaries. There are no tax implications.

Insurance

You should also inform the insurance companies involved of Edith's death and stop any direct debit payments currently being made to them. As Edith had a straight life policy, the company should pay out for the sum insured on proof of death, although the immediate payment depends on the value of the policy. Again, the type of policy dictates whether or not it is paid to the estate and therefore included in it for IHT purposes. However, building and content insurance should be continued and you would need to write to the company concerned.

Edith's life insurance and endowment policies had been taken out a long time ago. The endowment policy was 'with profits', which means that in addition to the paid-up value shown on the policy there is an additional 'bonus' sum to be paid. This additional amount depends on how well the insurance company's managers have done with their investments. In your letter to the insurance company you should give not only the policy numbers but also the actual value of the policies and dates of issue. In the case of the endowment policy you should ask what the 'with profits' value is. Depending on the type of insurance policy, some have a 'life' element written in so it is worth asking the company if this is the case.

Edith had not invested in a pension nor had she a company pension. Again, if she had you would have to write to the company concerned, notifying them of her death and asking for a precise valuation. They in turn would require proof of death and confirmation of your role as executor.

Bank and building society accounts

As James and Edith had held a joint deposit and current account you would not need to amend any normal payments that go through as a matter of course. Joint account holders can continue to withdraw from a jointly held account. However, for inheritance tax purposes you have to obtain a balance of each account at the date of death. That amount is usually halved, in the case of accounts held jointly by husband and wife or partner, and the proportion that belonged to the deceased will be put down on the Capital Taxes form. Accounts held by a single person would have to be noted at full value and payment into and out of these accounts would have to be stopped. Funds held in bank or building society accounts arc only released upon sight of a Grant of Probate or Letters of Administration, assuming they are not in joint names.

You should now be receiving payments (and bills). It might be worthwhile to open an executor's account at this stage, especially if other persons are going to benefit. A separate account is essential if you know the will is going to be contested. If there is considerable money coming in to the executor's account then it may be advantageous to open a savings account. This will ensure that your monies are kept apart from those of the estate. In addition, the statements from the bank are a useful record of monies and expenditure. Do ask the bank what charges are likely to apply. (This charge is deducted from the residue of the estate.)

Check with both banks and building societies where Edith held an account to see whether there is a second or third account not known to you. When visiting either organisation return any bank cards or passbooks held, obtaining a receipt for each.

There are billions of unclaimed funds held by banks and building societies where people have forgotten to supply details alongside their will or in a separate letter or document.

Shares and other investments

For a number of years Edith had dabbled on the stock market and had a variety of shares in her portfolio. You would have to locate the share certificates and on a separate sheet note the number and type of shares held (such as preferential or ordinary) and the names of each company found on individual certificates. (The same would apply for like investments, eg unit trusts, PEPs.) Obtain the *Financial Times* (or any of the major national daily papers) dated the day after Edith's death, and you should find buying and selling prices quoted. The value you are looking for is the lower of the two quoted, as you buy at a higher price and sell at a lower one. You value the shares by taking the lower of the two figures quoted in the *Stock Register* and adding one-quarter of the difference between the share's two prices. You can also value shares by subtracting the bid from the offer price and taking half of that figure and adding it to the lower of the quoted prices. These figures can be found in other publications; for example, the Stock Exchange publishes the *Daily Official List* and main libraries hold a copy of the *Stock Register*.

If the death occurs over a weekend, you can choose to value shares either on the basis of Friday's closing price or Monday's closing value. The lower price will, of course, result in less tax and possibly lower probate fees.

Of course, if you are unhappy about valuing shares yourself, you can ask the securities department of your bank to do this or telephone a stockbroker.

Example 4. Share value list

Number of shares held	Company	Price quoted	Value of holding
500	BW & Co Ltd	156/150	£757.50
600	KP Ordinary	172/160	£978.00
600	Plate & Co	148/140	£852.00
1,000	Copper Works	222/210	£2,130.00
800	Lampshade Ltd	170/163	£1,318.00

(Note: The names and prices above are examples only and do not relate to any known company.)

Most shares are quoted in pence. For instance, a value quoted at, say, 578 translates into £5 and 78 pence. Certain high-value shares, however, are quoted in pounds.

You may notice from the certificates that most dividend payments are made twice yearly, although this is not always the case. To find out whether any payment is due write to the company secretary of each company concerned on the *Register* and ask whether any dividends are due. If you can't find dividend vouchers, ask for these at the same time. Charges are normally made when providing this information. If you do not have the head office address of each company, then contact the Stock Exchange, as all quoted companies are registered there with their head office addresses noted on file.

Once a death has been notified to the Registrar, dividend payments are usually retained pending probate unless the shares are held jointly.

When checking the newspaper, you might have noticed that beside the quoted price a symbol or letters are shown. 'Xd' means that the price quoted excludes the dividend value. Usually, this is noted some two weeks or so before the dividend is due. So if Edith had sold the shares with the Xd in force, she would still receive the dividend on those shares and not the person who bought them. The price quoted is, therefore, lower to take this into account.

Dividend cheques are usually sent out on the day the dividend is due but prepared beforehand.

If a rights issue had been in force it would mean that the company is issuing new shares to existing shareholders at a price lower than the current market price. In this instance a letter is sent out to all shareholders and the proportion of shares offered is based on the number of existing shares held.

A scrip issue would be noted alongside the price. Exscrip means that it is the value placed on the share while the company is issuing new shares to existing shareholders based on the percentage of their existing holding.

Edith's portfolio had not included any unit trusts. If it had, you would have to write to the unit trust companies concerned. Unlike shares, where you hold a number of shares in a particular company, for a unit trust you hold units within a trust and that trust has a specified category of investment, say Small Company, Far East, Recovery and so on. These are usually quoted in the *Financial Times*. Basically, money put into a unit trust is 'pooled' with other investors' money in the same category of trust, to purchase shares in companies fulfilling that category's definition. Prices can also go up and down.

Personal Equity Plans (PEPs)

These were a popular form of investment. Until PEPs were discontinued, you could have put up to £6,000 per annum into a general PEP and £3,000 into a single-company PEP in any tax year. If the deceased owned a PEP and the estate continued to hold it in order to complete the year's investment, the above rules would apply to the date of death and interest after that date would be taxed as per a normal account.

From April 1999, no future PEPs can be taken out, but provided you do not withdraw from your own, you can continue to hold it as a tax-free investment. TESSAs also ceased at that time and any existing TESSAs became a TOSA.

Individual Savings Accounts (ISAs)

These were launched on 6 April 1999 replacing TESSAs and PEPs.

ISAs are supposed to be the tax-free savings plan for the next 10 years, ie any gain made is free from capital gains tax and any income is free from income tax but they are not free from IHT. Any income received from shares had a 10 per cent tax credit attached. This has now ceased to be a repayable sum. As with TESSAs and PEPs, investors must be 18 or over and be ordinarily resident in the United Kingdom. This age limit has been reduced to 16 but only for the purchase of mini-ISAs, ie not equity-based ones. This is because the equity market is deemed more risky.

The ISAs are split into what are called mini or cash ISAs and maxi ISAs, the latter being for equity-based investment. The limit for a maxi ISA is £7,200 and for a mini or cash ISA is £3,600, which can be invested in each tax year from 6 April to the following 5 April. You cannot have both a maxi or mini ISA taken out in the same tax year.

From October 2009, people over 50 with birthdays in that tax year will be able to avail themselves of the new rate of £10,200 a year for an equity ISA and £5,100 for a cash one. Those individuals under the age of 50 will have to wait until 6 April 2010 in order to benefit from this change in the allowances.

The Government has introduced a standard mark called CAT, which stands for Cost, Availability and Terms, and should now be looked at as the Government's standard of high performance. The CAT mark signifies that there are no hidden charges or penalties and that access to investors' money is easy.

Providers of ISAs have been rather slow off the mark because for one thing these investments are far more complicated than their predecessors. Select the ISA of your choice and while a CAT mark is extremely useful do ensure that past performance in other similar investments is also taken into consideration.

Other income

As she had not worked for many years, Edith had no income coming in other than the occasional dividend payment and interest from her building society accounts, deposit accounts and National Savings. You would still have to write to the Inspector of Taxes at the nearest HMRC office, notifying the office of her death and letting them know that the small amounts of income earned had either already been noted on James's income tax return form or noted on her own income tax return form.

Had Edith been a pensioner, then you would have to write, advising of Edith's death, to her Department of Social Security office, whose address can be found in the telephone directory.

Hire purchase

Should a hire purchase agreement or any other loan agreement including credit cards have been in force, you would have to write to the company concerned and ask for an exact assessment of the debt. In the meantime, if the agreement had been jointly signed, the surviving signatory should continue to pay the monthly instalments.

Forgotten accounts

Lost or forgotten assets often result when investors fail to keep a note of where all their investments are located. While National Savings have their own tracing service for lost bonds and accounts (tel: 0845 964 5000), forgotten bank or building society accounts mean a letter to each and every organisation, unless you use the Unclaimed Assets Register who will do it for a fee.

A new Act was passed in 2007 which means that if an account has remained untouched for 15 years, ie dormant, then the state will be able to claim the money unless the bank or building society has already signed up to the Voluntary Scheme where the money goes to a central fund and then is passed onto various charities. The only exemption is where a customer has a 'no mail' account, ie has asked not to be contacted in writing.

This is a worrying development and will be a significant earner for the Treasury. It has a wide range covering other investments such as fixed term accounts and Cash ISAs. It is therefore very important to keep an accurate note of your investments and to ensure that you do move money in and out of the account or investment.

Listing the valuations

Most of the contents of the house had been jointly owned with no hire purchase scheme. Therefore, it would be a matter of listing all items and placing an approximate second-hand value against each. For antiques and collectables, a specialist dealer should be asked for a probate valuation. A family car, for instance, valued at £1,000 would be apportioned to her estate at £500, in other words half the value. Should an amount of the loan still be outstanding against it, then if jointly owned, the appropriate apportionment would need to be deducted.

As the jewellery had already been itemised in her will this need not be done, but the full probate valuation would have to be placed on the valuation sheet as Edith owned the jewellery outright. General items, such as clothes, tables, chairs, TV and so on, would not need itemising but, again, a second-hand value would have to be noted. HMRC does not expect an exact and absolute value for each of these items down to the last pound but does expect a valuation that is sensible and realistic. Again, these general items, if jointly owned, have half of each value listed. As an example of inclusions on an inventory list, see pages 157–58.

Any cash in Edith's possession at the time of her death, whether in her handbag or in her desk drawer at home, would have to be accounted for on the valuation sheet. This loose cash could be used on the estate's behalf to purchase stamps, for example, provided it is accounted for. Any money spent personally on the funeral could be reimbursed from the estate once probate has been granted. On the other hand, if there is sufficient cash in a bank savings account, then with the production of a bill as well as the death certificate the bank will often settle the bill before probate but only directly with the funeral home.

Let us assume that the estate, once valued, exceeds the first valuation figure. As this is only your rough guide it would not matter. What does matter, however, is that the value on the Capital Taxes form is correct.

With all the valuations to hand, the forms can be completed. At this stage, if it is applicable, ie on the death of the second spouse or civil partner with at least a portion of the unused nil rate band being possible to claim and with the estate being in excess of the IHT threshold, then the forms can be completed. In addition to the usual IHT200 or IHT205, in the above instance you would also need to complete the IHT216 and the D18 which the CTO will return to you or the Registrar in order for probate to be granted.

In the meantime, while awaiting probate or letters of administration, you should continue to administer the estate where possible. Once probate has been granted you should commence collection and/or sale of any assets and payments of any debts, keeping an account of all transactions in your book-keeping journal. Remember that until probate is granted, you legally cannot distribute any assets in the estate.

Administering a trust

Trusts have only been briefly mentioned because of their diversity and individuality. There will usually be more than one trustee and the likelihood is that at least one will belong to a profession, such as a solicitor or accountant. Trusts should state whether or not trustees in a profession or business will be able to charge for their time and any incurred expenses.

Some trusts are simple and therefore quite easy to deal with, while the reverse is also true. However, the principles of investing a trust's assets are similar whether a trust has £100,000 or £500,000 to invest. What does matter is keeping the trust's expenses to a minimum, keeping accurate records of the financial affairs of the trust and investing in financial markets that are able to produce a reasonable income, but as important is to safeguard capital and its growth from unsafe investments and underlying inflation. Advice on investments should be taken.

The following paragraphs are only meant as a general guide. In most instances a trust is written so that it is within the Trustees Act, which is there to protect the trust's assets and ultimately the beneficiaries. It allows for a certain proportion of money to be held in a narrow range band of investments with the remainder in a broad range band. It does not allow for speculative, risky investments such as commodity futures. Should a trust be written outside the confines of this Act, then as a beneficiary or one of the trustees it would be recommended that you seek independent legal advice. The trustees are by law obliged to follow exactly the wishes of a trust.

As a trustee, before considering investing monies for the trust, examine the following carefully. What does the trust state? What are the life tenant's and residuary beneficiaries' wishes? What are their ages and needs? What has the will specified? For example, should the life tenant be an elderly person, ie over 80 years of age, or a person with a disability then long-term investment bonds bought over par (ie at a capital loss) would perhaps be unsuitable. Would the residuary beneficiaries be interested to continue any long-term government bonds after the death of the life tenant? What is the value of assets in the trust? Has capital appreciation or specific income been stated in the will? And do the proposed investments allow for this? Does the life tenant need the extra income? Are any of the trustees life tenants or residuary beneficiaries? Remember, expenses and underlying inflation can erode a trust's investments.

If there is any doubt as to a trustee's impartiality or should there have been any possible illegal acts, then the residuary beneficiary and the other beneficiaries may be able to sue the trustees for any loss. The trustee has the fiduciary responsibility to the trust.

Under the new self-assessment rules, each trustee can make a return and in turn each will be liable for any errors or omissions made that result in any loss of tax due to HMRC.

11

What Happens in Scotland?

Changes were made on 1 August 1995 when the Requirements of Writing (Scotland) Act 1995 came into force. Prior to this Act, wills fell into two categories: holograph wills and attested wills. The former were written by the testator's hand and usually not witnessed, and the latter will was either handwritten or typed and witnessed by two witnesses. As holograph wills were not probative then affidavit evidence must prove it was written in the testator's hand.

For all wills written after 1 August 1995 the rules under the above Act must be followed. Details of these can be found on the HMRC website, manual page 12047.

In most cases you will have had prior notice of your task as executor. However, it is worth noting at the outset that in Scotland, except where an estate does not exceed £30,000 gross and is known as a small estate (see below), in the majority of cases a solicitor's service or that of a licensed executing practitioner is used. This chapter, therefore, briefly notes procedures in Scotland, explaining the different terminology used, and highlights areas of major differences.

The first thing to do after the death, wherever you live in the United Kingdom, is to find the will. It may have been lodged with the deceased's bank or solicitor, or hidden away at the family home. Although a photocopy of a will cannot be substituted for the original – except for an action of a declarator to prove the terms of the will, where the original document has been lost, brought in the Court of Session – it is advisable to have a photocopy for your own reference.

What is a 'small estate'?

In Scotland a special procedure is followed if an estate is under £30,000 gross. The legal term for this size of estate is a *small estate*. For estates that exceed this value this involves, in intestate cases, a petition to the court for appointment of an *'executor dative'*. Presentation (inventory of estate and petition) is rarely made by personal application; instead, it is presented by a solicitor or a licensed executing practitioner.

The staff at the Commissary Offices throughout Scotland will process small estates provided that complications do not arise. If they are able to assist, they require full and detailed information regarding the estate and its assets. In calculating the value of the estate, debts such as funeral expenses, gas or electricity bills, hire purchase payments and any outstanding mortgage must be disregarded. The applicant must supply information to the staff at the Commissary Office, making a list and supporting this list by documentation. All property must be included in this list, even accounts held jointly.

In addition to a list of assets, you would also have to supply a death certificate, a divorce certificate, if applicable, and a will. If there is no will, the court will appoint the closest relative in order of 'preferred' status, namely spouse, child, brother or sister, parent.

As in England, there is no charge made by the Sheriff Clerk in giving advice or information or for completing the inventory or forms on an applicant's behalf. Again as in England, there is a statutory fee charged whether a solicitor is used or not and this is calculated on the basis of the gross value of the estate. For an estate of £5,000 or under no fee is charged and where the gross value is £5,001 and above the fee is £90 for personal applications or £40 in solicitors' cases.

Will you give him a future?

Leave a legacy of hope

Mark felt life was closing in on him. One day he had his own business and was living happily with his wife and daughter, the next he had lost everything. He felt he couldn't go on. **"Without Bethany, I wouldn't be alive today"** he says.

Bethany Christian Trust makes a difference in the lives of hundreds of people like Mark every day. We get alongside people who are homeless and vulnerable and work with them to overcome the underlying causes of their homelessness as well as helping deal with their immediate needs.

Our services help people get back on their feet and live independently; we offer hurting people hope and a future.

Please leave a legacy of hope today by writing Bethany into your will. For more information call 0131 625 5320 or email info@bethanyct.com.

Bethany Christian Trust is a registered charity no SC003783. "Scottish Charity of the Year 2009".

FundRaising
Standards Board

In all intestate cases other than a surviving spouse case you will be asked to obtain a *bond of caution* (type of insurance policy against any mistakes or misappropriation of the funds) from an insurance company before you are able to take on the task.

Information needed

Bank and building society accounts

The passbooks must be presented to the companies for updating. Any interest accrued up to the date of death must be noted by the manager in pencil. If you cannot find a passbook, write to the bank or building society concerned and ask them to supply you with a letter stating the type of account, the account number and the value plus interest, noted separately.

Insurance policies

The insurance company must be asked to supply details of the policy, its value, its number and any bonuses applicable.

National Savings Bank (including National Savings certificates)

A letter must be obtained from the Director of Savings giving the value of each holding, including interest, up to the date of death. This address will be found on the reverse of the claim form, which you obtain from your local post office. (National Savings, Marton, Blackpool FY3 9YP. Tel: 0845 964 5000.)

Premium Bonds

If the actual bonds cannot be produced, then the holder's registration number should be given. If this also cannot be found, write to the address on page 161 and ask for confirmation of the numbers, stating why you need them.

Stocks and shares

The valuation route as found on pages 163–64 needs to be followed and should include the value of the item, plus dividends. If a stockbroker or bank is used, ask them to confirm these details in writing.

Heritable property

This includes a house, shop, land, etc. A valuation from an estate agent, solicitor or other appropriate person must be obtained, again in writing. It is advisable, where heritable property forms part of an estate, for a solicitor's services to be used.

Rights

There are two rights given: first, prior rights, and second, legal rights. Prior rights take precedence over all other rights of succession in either a fully or a partially intestate estate where spouse or civil partners are entitled to both prior and legal rights. An exemption in respect of assets taken by a spouse or civil partner is allowed by way of prior rights. Prior rights means just that – the spouse has a right to the property and these rights must be satisfied before legal rights; legal rights allow for what is legally available to a spouse or descendant after deductions such as funeral, IHT, administrative payments, ie net moveable estate; see the following pages for further clarification.

Once you are sure that all the information and its supportive evidence is to hand, you need to arrange an interview with the Commissary Office. At the end of the interview all offices require that you make a declaration that the information given by you is 'full and true'. If the deceased died intestate, in some offices you would need to bring two witnesses to the interview to swear on your behalf that you are who you say you are and that your relationship to the deceased is as you say. One witness must not be related to either the deceased or the applicant and the other witness, although a relative is allowable, must not be a beneficiary.

Tax forms

There were four tax forms in Scotland which doubled as an inventory of estate on which confirmation is granted.

The forms have now been amalgamated into one standard form entitled C1 which covers all estate inventory.

To obtain the relevant Capital Taxes Office and commissary forms, you should contact the Probate and Inheritance Tax helpline on the Capital Taxes Office. In Scotland form C1 (C3 is the relevant booklet) and C5 once completed will be forwarded by the Capital Taxes Office to the Commissary Office.

Estate checklist

An estate checklist, reproduced by courtesy of the Commissary Office in Edinburgh, is shown below. Indeed, this list could be used as a guide for those preparing an inventory of an estate in England, Wales or Northern Ireland. It is stressed, however, that this list is not exhaustive, merely an indication of how detailed the inventory should be. Details of each item, along with its current value at date of death, should accompany the list:

Bank and building society accounts including Post Office Giro
Insurance policies
Premium Bonds
Savings bonds (including index-linked 'Granny bonds')
National Savings certificates
Old age pension
Invalidity pension
DSS death grant
Pension from employer
Holiday pay outstanding
Salary outstanding
Employer's death grant (gratuity)
Employer's superannuation
Mobility allowance
Shares, including those in co-operatives
Stocks and shares (eg Treasury Stock, consolidated and public stock, etc)
Repayment of TV licence stamps

Overpayment of rent, council tax (including rebates)
Gift vouchers
Estate abroad
Trust estate
Income from a trust
Rents from property
Beneficiary under someone else's will
Personal effects
Motor car
Cash in hand (including in hospital, nursing home, etc)
Income tax repayment
Royalties
Repayment of club subscriptions (and motoring organisations)
Repayment of loans to clubs
House, garage
Business
Strip of land
Feu duty (superiority): Ground burdens
Livestock

What does it all mean?

It is important to understand what is meant by certain legal words and phrases as some of these differ between Scotland and England. For example, in Scotland, what is meant by 'the house' or 'the furnishings' in the context of the surviving spouse's prior rights? The house is the home of the deceased in which the surviving spouse was in residence at the date of death. Furnishings mean any item of furniture owned by the deceased not including cars, jewellery or money. The house up to £300,000 goes to the surviving spouse or surviving civil partner, provided the value is there, and there are children of the deceased. It is worth remembering that with all 'rights' in intestacy cases, where there are other relations such as surviving parents, and brothers and sisters with issue, this can change what is paid by the deceased person's estate.

Should a will have been written appointing you as an executor, you would be referred to as an '*executor nominate*'. As in England, if you find that you cannot fulfil your appointment for one reason or another you would have to sign a statement officially declining your role. You might be the only executor and, if so, you must ask another person to act as executor and you must wait until he or she assumes this role before resigning from your office.

In Scotland, if a person dies without a will, the court appoints an executor known as an '*executor dative*'. Just as in England, the duty of an executor dative is to collect, administer and distribute the assets according to the intestacy laws.

There are two types of estate: heritable (meaning house, buildings, land) and moveable (meaning furniture, cash, etc). An estate usually has both, as the majority of people now own their own home.

The final value of a house is determined once any outstanding debts, ie mortgage or home improvement loan, have been paid. If the deceased has died intestate, then the value of the house up to £300,000 goes to the surviving spouse. Settlement of prior rights reduces the value of the fund from the net moveable estate upon which the legal rights amount is based, but prior rights do not affect legal rights other than in this way.

If the intestate estate does not have the value in it to meet the prior rights, then the spouse or surviving civil partner may be entitled to the whole estate. In cases involving partial intestacy cases, any legacies bequeathed to and accepted by spouse or civil partner are deducted from cash provision: see above.

If a house has a survivorship destination clause in the title deeds, whoever is the survivor of this clause inherits the property; see 'Heritable property'.

Children

Prior to 26 November 1968 a child born out of a marriage and not mentioned specifically in a will could not normally inherit from his or her parents if the beneficiaries of the will were referred to as 'my children'. The illegitimate child could only claim legal rights if the will was executed on or after 26 November 1968, and refers to 'children'. Illegitimate children are included unless, for instance, there is reference such as to 'lawful children'.

The legal application of the word 'child' or 'children' in Scotland refers to children of a marriage, adopted children and now illegitimate children *but not* stepchildren. For stepchildren to be included in distribution of an estate the will has specifically to state the legacy along with the child's name.

A child under 16 cannot legally accept a legacy him or herself. Rather, the legacy has to be given to the parents or guardians on the child's behalf for the purpose of investing, but only in secure investments. The parents or guardians would have to sign the receipt for the legacy.

Once the child has reached the age of 16 years, he or she would be able to receive the entire legacy, including any interest earned.

Heritable property

If a property is owned by two people with the title deed drawn to include a survivorship destination clause, despite what is written in the will the house will automatically pass to the surviving owner without the property included in the confirmation to the deceased's estate. However, this does not apply if the destination has been recalled by the deceased in his or her lifetime, or if the deceased had provided the whole purchase price. In such cases the property must be confirmed and the title transferred by the executors to the heir.

Where property is bequeathed to a person under a will, or where it is passing to a person under the intestate succession rules, the title to the property can be transferred to the executors by signing a document appropriately called a 'docket'. A solicitor or licensed executing practitioner would have to draw one up for you.

A docket contains the name(s) of the executor(s), the name of the deceased, and the name of the person to whom the property is being transferred. It has also to state what rights are involved, ie whether he or she has prior rights or legal rights to the property and whether it is part of the gift as noted in the will. The full address of the house must also be included. If the house is going to be sold, a document granting legal title to the purchaser called a 'disposition' will have to be prepared, again by a solicitor or licensed conveyancing practitioner.

Intestate estate

Before 1964 the intestacy rules regarding the distribution to the surviving spouse and children were somewhat unfair. However, in 1964 the Succession (Scotland) Act effectively altered the existing intestacy rules.

Where there is a surviving spouse, by right he or she is entitled to be the sole administrator of the estate. If the estate exceeds the prior rights, then other entitled persons may act.

There are two further terms, already mentioned, peculiar to Scottish law: 'prior rights' and 'legal rights'. 'Prior rights' means that the surviving spouse has a 'right' to the deceased's house. The value of items under prior rights are as follows: house up to £300,000; furniture £24,000 (excluding the car); and a cash right (paid out of the heritable estate and the moveable estate) worth £42,000 if there was issue, and £75,000 if there was no issue.

If there is an outstanding balance on the mortgage, the surviving spouse receives the value of the house less any outstanding mortgage. This is so even if an endowment policy formed part of the estate to pay off the mortgage upon death.

Where the furnishings of the house exceed £24,000, the surviving spouse is entitled to choose furnishings up to the value of £24,000. Again, the value received is limited to the value in the estate.

It is worth noting that a car, jewellery or money are not included in the term 'furnishings' and furnishings do not necessarily have to be located in the deceased person's home.

After prior rights have been satisfied then 'legal rights' apply. Legal rights are taken from that part of the estate that remains after debts and prior rights have been paid.

In Scotland, even with a will, you cannot absolutely exclude your spouse or children from inheriting part of your moveable estate, as they have a 'legal right' to part of it. If a spouse and children survive, the spouse takes one-third and the children one-third. If there is a surviving spouse but no children, then the spouse takes half. If there is no surviving spouse, the children take half. Only the remaining one-third or one-half of the estate may be disposed of by the testator. However, the heritable estate may be disposed of as the testator wishes.

The estate that remains after both prior rights and legal rights have been satisfied is known as 'free estate'. This portion is distributed according to the laws of intestate succession to the children or to other relatives of the deceased.

The order of succession to the free estate is (1) children; (2) parents/brother and sister (equal share of the estate); (3) brothers or sisters if there are no parents or (4) parents if there are no brothers or sisters; (5) surviving spouse; (6) uncles, aunts; (7) other living traceable family members generation by generation. If a member of a particular category predeceased the deceased leaving issue, such issue share their parents' entitlement. If he or she dies leaving a surviving spouse or civil partner but without children, parent, brother, sister or issue of brother or sister then the surviving spouse or civil partner has the whole estate. If no relative can be traced, despite extensive searches by the executor dative, the estate goes to the Crown once all expenses and debts have been paid.

Does divorce alter a will?

In England if a person makes out a will and then subsequently marries and divorces, the granting of the 'decree absolute' will make the will invalid unless the will was made out in contemplation of marriage and states that fact and the person's name. Furthermore, a divorce does not now render the will invalid but it is read as if the ex-spouse had died immediately before the deceased. In Scotland, however, this does not apply; neither marriage nor divorce invalidates a will.

An interesting point arises from this. If you do not make out a new will setting aside gifts or money to your new spouse, he or she will not benefit under your old will. There is a way around this, however. The new spouse can claim legal rights which would entitle him or her to one-third (or if you have no children, one-half) but of the moveable estate only. He or she could not claim the house.

Under intestacy, divorced spouses or civil partners take no interest in the estate of the former spouse or civil partner. Where a degree of judicial separation has been made, the husband does not inherit any of the wife's intestate estate which she acquired after separation but there is no similar rule barring a separated wife inheriting.

Debts

There are three categories of debt in Scotland: 'secured debts' (ie overdraft, mortgage), 'privileged debts' (funeral expenses, council tax) and 'ordinary debts' (butcher, baker and candlestick maker). You can pay secure debts and privileged debts as and when the money is available, but ordinary debts have to wait until the estate is finalised, usually six months after the date of death.

For the purpose of division of the estate, a debt can only be applied to its equivalent source of estate. In other words, a loan against the house (heritable) can only be set against that source. Similarly, expenses such as telephone bills and funeral expenses must be paid out of the moveable estate.

This is where matters start to get complicated: calculating the net moveable estate or heritable property and working out the legal rights and so on. It is, therefore, not within the scope of this book to elucidate further and you would be well advised to involve a solicitor or licensed executing practitioner in practice in Scotland. Assistance on matters pertaining to Scotland can be best obtained in the first instance by contacting the HMRC Helpline on 0845 3020900 or visiting the website www.hmrc.gov.uk and going to the manuals section, referring to IHTM1200 – Succession contents. For useful addresses in Scotland, see Appendix 4.

12

Winding Up an Estate

The first thing that usually crosses an executor's mind is the release of the house. As more and more people are now purchasing their own home this usually means that there is a mortgage to consider. For mortgages that are linked to insurance policies the amount outstanding on death is automatically paid off providing it is not an endowment policy.

Property

The first thing that has to be looked at is the title of the house. If it is in joint ownership, then it usually (but not always) passes to the survivor. You should consult your solicitor, building society or bank if they hold the deeds in order to establish the exact position, and a charge to the estate for this service will be made. However, if the house is going to a named beneficiary, then, in certain instances, the building society or bank may agree to that person taking over the existing mortgage or remortgaging the house.

If there are not sufficient assets for distribution, you might have to put the house up for sale. Once it has been sold and the mortgage paid off, then the remaining amount can be distributed. Upon request, the building society or bank will let you know the amount outstanding on the mortgage.

The Land Registry notes all property transactions throughout the United Kingdom. The Registry has details of approximately 19 million registered properties in England and Wales and estimates that there are further properties still to be registered. The Land Registration Act 2002 and Land Registration Rules 2003 came into force in October 2003, replacing the law for land registration, which was the first time in 75 years. The Acts, amended in 2005, lay out procedures and rules. There has been a subsequent amendment as of July 2009 specially relating to fees and charges. Obviously, if the property that you are concerned with is not registered, then the Land Registry holds no information. To find out if the property is registered, the Registry has a series of maps called the Public Index Map, which not only tells you if the property is registered but shows the extent of land in every registered title. This Map is open to inspection but fees are now payable. It is worthwhile noting that anyone can obtain information on a property that is registered, even if they are not the owners.

As executor, once probate has been given, you have to notify the Land Registry (offices in most towns and large cities; see your local telephone directory for the one nearest you or go on to the Land Registry website, www.landregistry.gov.uk) that the title of the property is now transferred to the ownership of the executors, in other words the estate. The house can be transferred directly to one of the beneficiaries but a further application has to be made to the Registry and perhaps to HMRC also.

The Land Registry form can be obtained by asking for Form AS1 Assent or Approbation or for TRI for transfers from either the Land Registry office nearest to you or from the Law Stationers Office or online. If you are using the services of a solicitor this process will be undertaken on your behalf.

You should note on the ASI form the title number, the address of the property concerned, the date, the names of the executors (and their addresses) as well as the name and address of the deceased. The form must be witnessed, with the witness supplying his or her full address and occupation.

In rare instances a half share of a property may be transferred to the other joint owner with an agreement drawn up to state that the person can continue to live in that abode, known as an interest in possession. So despite giving it away, if interest in possession exists this half share still has to be accounted for on the inheritance tax forms less, of course, any liabilities. For inheritance tax, interest in possession (IIP) is seen as an ineffective transfer and the seven-year rule would not apply, ie the total of the property has to be included. New rules on IIP were introduced on 22 March 2006. Seek advice from your tax adviser or solicitor on how the changes might affect your will trust.

Land Registry fees

The Land Registry charges a fee based on the value of the house whether the house has been transferred to the beneficiary or bought outright. This fee is known as Scale 2.

Table 12.1 – Land Registry Scale 2 charges from 6 July 2009

£0–£100,000	£50
£100,001–£200,000	£70
£200,001–£500,000	£90
£500,001–£1,000,000	£130
£1,000,001 and above	£260

What to do if you cannot find a title deed or know the title number

If you are unable to locate a title deed or a mortgage certificate and you doubt whether the house is registered, you should go to the Land Registry, where you should be able to inspect details pertaining to the property. Upon proof of your role as executor and proof that the property has no charge against it, the Land Registry would be able to send a replacement of the lost title deed. As registration of titles is still continuing, it may be that your property is not noted on the

Public Index map. This is still possible as compulsory registration has only been introduced relatively recently. Indeed, in
certain areas it means that some houses that have not been
sold have not been registered.

Among the deceased's papers there may be a copy of the original conveyance sent by the solicitor at the time the house was
purchased. This conveyance was the official document transferring ownership from the previous owner to the deceased. If
there is no record at the Land Registry and no conveyance document, then a visit to the street on which the property is located
might yield information as to who owns it. In the case of leasehold property the conveyance is called an assignment.

Transferring ownership

Once you have this deed, you are able to prepare a document
transferring ownership, whether as instructed in the will or as
administrator in the case of intestacy. Again, as with the normal
transfer of a registered property, the building society or bank
will give back the title deed to the property once the mortgage
has been repaid. Attached to the mortgage deed will be an
acknowledgement stating that the money has been paid off and
the mortgage discharged. This deed will also include a copy of
the deed of conveyance when the house was originally
purchased by the deceased.

In order to make up an assent, the title deeds must accompany the deed of conveyance along with the original grant of
probate or administration. On the assent form you need to
show the full details pertaining to the property, ie full address,
the name and full address of the person to whom the property
is being transferred, legal proof that the person died, the date of
death and the date that probate was granted. When returned to
you, the forms are said to be 'assented'. This assent form
should always be kept with the title deeds to the property.

A house held in joint ownership, ie as joint tenants passing
by survivorship, is more straightforward and no assent should
be needed. A death certificate is proof that the survivor is now

entitled to the property along with the deeds and should be sufficient. However, if you are the beneficiary yourself, you are, in effect, writing an assent to yourself. If you are representing a number of people, then an assent form should be used.

From August 2006, with the changes to the format of leases, the Land Registry has updated the 3.5 million existing leaseholders registers in easements in order to make it easier for the lay person to understand.

Leasehold property

The 'landlord' or leaseholder of leasehold property has to be notified that an assent is being done and may charge a fee, but this depends on the terms of the lease. He or she may also be entitled to retain a copy of the assent. On the form all details of the lease have to be noted, such as its length, what costs are attributed to it, etc.

Leasehold property starts its life usually with 99 years noted on the title deeds. As time marches on so the lease's expiry date comes closer to completion. When this occurs the property reverts back to the owner (or landlord) of the lease, but until that time you own the leasehold property and can sell it on. However, the owner of the freehold on the property has to be informed of any lease transfer taking place. The same form as for the transfer of ownership of freehold property is used.

When the beneficiary eventually comes to sell the house the original grant of probate, along with the assent, may need to be shown to prove legal ownership.

Because these property transfers can be fraught with danger when the beneficiary comes to sell – especially if the property is unregistered – it would be best to approach a solicitor and ask him or her to deal with matters. Instances have occurred when, at the final stage of selling a house, the purchaser's solicitor has noted that the property had not been legally transferred and the sale has been halted.

Bookkeeping

As an executor, it is your duty to keep a careful record of all amounts of money, property and any outstanding debts. This naturally necessitates bookkeeping.

You should keep a ledger noting all the amounts of money paid out, such as funeral expenses, telephone calls, train fares, petrol, stationery, even down to the last postage stamp. Keep a receipt for each item of expenditure and cross-reference this receipt with the same number noted in the ledger. Assets that have been sold in preparation for distribution should be noted on a separate page, stating when and to whom they were sold, the amount received for each item and where the money is now.

Money could be held on deposit and, if so, any interest payments received must also be included.

Dividend payments should also be noted along with any shares or other investments that have subsequently been sold. All of these will have vouchers which must be kept safely and again cross-referenced to the ledger.

Any tax that has been deducted from dividends or interest payments must be noted on your ledger, as eventually a repayment situation could arise.

It cannot be stressed too often that accurate and detailed books need to be kept. As an executor you can be asked up to 12 years after the date your duty first commenced to show what payments were received and what distributions were made. If you keep accurate accounts it is unlikely that any charge of maladministration can be levied against you.

It is a good idea to keep back a certain amount of money in case further payments need to be made, but, more importantly, it keeps the estate liquid. There is a further example of the benefit in doing this. Suppose there is an existing business and the expenses of that business are higher than the interest being received. If there is no liquidity, certain assets may have to be sold and the best possible price may not be obtained. Another example is that a beneficiary might need payment before final distribution takes place or perhaps creditors may need an interim or complete payment.

By keeping accurate accounts you can quickly pull together all the transactions once completion has taken place and the final winding-up procedure account-wise will be relatively simple.

Tax returns

As executor of the estate you are responsible for completing income tax returns on the estate's behalf. As there is no individual concerned after the date of death, then no personal tax relief is granted. For income tax purposes, the only relief that an estate can claim back is if it has had to obtain a loan from a bank in order to pay inheritance tax or the probate fee.

Before distribution, you have to fill in an income tax return form showing your calculation of how much tax is due based on the income received. This form should be signed and returned to HMRC which, if it agrees with it, will send you a demand for the estate tax due. Once this tax has been paid, distribution can take place. Always ask HMRC for a receipt of any tax paid as proof of the discharge of the estate's income tax liability.

When completing the income tax return you need to insert the period of administration. It is to be hoped that the winding-up procedure will not take longer than a year, but for each new tax year it enters, a new income tax return form must be filled in.

Any shares or unit trusts that have been sold must be included on this form and show what profit exists, if any, per share holding.

If the shares have risen in value, then you have to show the gain. Alongside the details write the phrase 'exempt £9,600', which refers to the amount of annual allowable capital gain before tax. (For tax year 2009/10 this exemption rises to £10,100 and for trustees it increases to £5,050.) Any loss that has been made can be set off against any other capital gain that the estate might have made.

Once the tax forms have been filled in they should be returned to HMRC, along with a letter formally giving notice that the administration of the estate has been closed, and giving the exact date when the completion of the estate occurred. As there may be residuary beneficiaries of the will you can ask for a tax form, R185E, to be sent to you on their behalf. One form per person is needed. Remember to ask for confirmation that HMRC has closed the estate's file and ask that any dividend folios sent to them are returned, as you will need these as evidence when preparing the final distribution.

The forms should then be returned to you together with any repayment. But it is one thing to owe HMRC money and quite another to collect it. HMRC asks you to pay within 30 days.

Accounts

After gaining probate, all assets and liabilities can be settled and on doing this the estate is considered to be complete. The legacies can now be distributed.

Should you have incurred expenses as executor you will now be able to reimburse yourself out of the executorship bank account. If the will states that executors should be paid for their time, then that account can also be settled.

All beneficiaries should now receive a letter from you stating that the estate is ready for distribution and that their legacy can be collected.

Distributing legacies

As an executor you are responsible for ensuring that there are no loose ends. Therefore, each legacy that is handed over to the beneficiary must be signed for. The receipt should contain the following:

(a) details of the sum of money or description of the legacy;
(b) full details of the estate's executors and who the deceased was;
(c) who the gift was given to under the terms of the deceased's will;
(d) the signature of the person who received the legacy.

A copy of this receipt should be kept for your records and the other copy retained by the beneficiary.

A slight problem arises if a beneficiary is under the age of 18. Legally a child cannot sign a receipt. In order to overcome this problem, the father or mother or lawful guardian should sign on the child's behalf with the proviso that when the beneficiary reaches the age of majority he or she will receive the money or gift plus any interest earned.

It is worth noting that a child under the age of 18 can also receive an income tax allowance as a single person. So it is not tax efficient for any sums of money to be placed in savings accounts where tax is deducted at source unless the interest earned in a year is likely to exceed £6,475 (2009/10). Banks and building societies now automatically deduct basic rate tax from monies held with them unless a form is signed that states that you are not liable to tax and therefore no tax should be deducted. You or the child's guardian should contact the HMRC repayment office at Belfast. A repayment claims form would need to be completed. Alternatively, you could open an account where money is paid gross and not net; for example, with National Savings accounts.

Once all the pecuniary legacies have been paid, the executor can re-examine whether any creditors have been overlooked or, for that matter, anything of relevance to the estate. Any specific legacy, such as a specified chair or painting, or a piece of jewellery, can now be given. Remember to have a receipt signed by the person who is inheriting the legacy. The time should be used for double-checking that everything that should have been done has been done. Once you are happy that this is the case then final accounts can be prepared.

Final accounts

If the bookkeeping has been done accurately it will be a straightforward matter to pull all the accounts together. Each sheet of accounts should be clearly headed, noting the period of administration, the deceased person's name and the type of account to be found on the sheet.

Capital accounts

The first and prime account sheet is the capital account. On one side this shows what the asset values were on the date of death, eg property less outstanding mortgage, the value of any life insurance policies, pension premiums, building society or bank accounts, National Savings, shares, retirement pensions and so on. It itemises all assets and their value and then any debts, noted on the other side of the sheet, are deducted from this amount.

With the increase in 'buy to let' properties, it is worth noting here that should a property be rented out, any income received on that property has also to be returned, less any allowable expenditure. The deceased's residence cannot be let out to a third party by the executor in the hope of reducing the value of the residence, as this would not be accepted by the Capital Taxes Office.

Debts that include probate fees, inheritance tax, bank charges, Land Registry fee and so on have also to be noted.

Looking at the last bank statement, you should see if the amount agrees with the total amount shown in your calculations. If so, this is the final and true account. If not, then you must go over the accounts again until they are reconciled.

Income account

The income account is the next sheet that needs to be completed. It should include any income received throughout the period of administration – in other words, any dividends that have been paid, any profits paid on the trust, any interest paid on the bank account, etc, less the amount of tax deducted at source. Not only are receipts shown in the income account but also any payments that have been made; for example, mortgage repayment. The final figure shown should match exactly the final figure given on the income tax return form.

Also to be included on the income account sheet is any tax repayment made to the estate.

Distributions sheet

The last sheet to be completed is the distributions sheet. Again, all details pertaining to the estate need to be noted.

At the top of the sheet insert the remaining amount of money still held by the estate. This figure will be found in the capital account sheet. All payments made out to the beneficiaries need to be itemised, even if they include a house and contents, shares or unit trusts or the residue in the bank account. Each beneficiary in receipt of a legacy must have his or her name and what he or she is receiving noted here and its value. The total figure should match exactly with the receipts brought across from the capital and income sheets.

The closing stages

It is recommended that the distribution of the estate, unless it is a small and uncomplicated one, should not be completed in under a six-month period. This is because a claimant can come forward up to six months from the date probate was granted. There are special circumstances where the time limit may be extended by the court.

If the estate has already been distributed, the executors could be looking at a court case whereby the claimant can state that he or she was not treated equally or that his or her claim was not considered when it should have been.

Once all the accounts have been written up, the beneficiaries are entitled to have the opportunity to study them, if they so wish. They might have certain questions regarding the distribution, tax or interest payment; all need to be answered. When each beneficiary has seen the accounts and agreed them, each person must sign the bottom of all account sheets.

Once cheques have been given to the beneficiaries and your receipts filed safely away, write to the bank advising that all payments have been made and that the executorship account should now be closed. Usually banks charge fees for handling administrative work. This fee will be deducted from the money held in the account. Whatever money is left is given to the residuary beneficiary unless there is a life interest (trust).

All papers together with the signed copy of the account should be placed in a safe place along with the probate certificates.

Example 1. Capital accounts

Estate accounts covering the period of administration from date of death 27 April 2008 to 30 September 2008.

Receipts	£
Somerset Farm	285,000
Contents	5,450
Antiques	10,950
Jewellery	5,250
Stamp collection	6,800
National Savings certificates	8,000
Building society account (1)	5,000
Building society account (2)	2,500
Half share of bank account	150
Premium Bonds	500
Life insurance policy	25,000
Endowment policy (with profits)	15,500
Stocks and shares (see separate list)	15,000
Cash	400
	385,500
Interest paid on building society accounts	150
Gain on shares sold	2,050
Interest on National Savings	200
	387,900

Less Payments	£
Funeral account	2,250
Probate fee	90
Bank charges	35
Executor's expenses	145
Debts outstanding at death	2,000
Solicitor's fees	2,600
Legacies paid	1,000

IHT should be noted here had the estate been liable.

Debts paid from the estate	8,120
Balance of estate to distribution account	379,780

(Note £1,000 of legacy has already been paid)

Signatures:

Executor . . . .   Approved by . . . .

Date . . . .

Note: The figures shown are approximations.

* The Inheritance Tax Threshold applies at the rate at date of death, ie 40 per cent – £325,000 (2009/10).

Appendix 1
Probate Checklist

1. Register death and obtain death certificate (additional copies if necessary) from the nearest Registrar of Births, Deaths and Marriages.
2. If the deceased left instructions for organ donation, make sure that this request is passed on to the medical staff.
3. If directed under the will, consider funeral arrangements.
4. Collect the will. Obtain photocopies. If the deceased died intestate, consider whether you want to apply to administer the estate. If so, obtain the necessary forms from the Personal Applications Department of the nearest Probate Registry.
5. Do you need a grant of probate for an existing will or letters of administration in the case of intestacy? Ask the Probate Registry to send you the forms.
6. Collect details of all assets and liabilities for valuation purposes. Write off to relevant institutions including banks confirming the death, your position and asking for a valuation up to the date of death and whether tax has been deducted. If the estate is insolvent see a solicitor immediately.
7. Prepare a valuation sheet for the approximate value of all items in the estate. Start bookkeeping ledgers.

8. Ascertain from your valuation sheet whether or not the estate is valued at £325,000 or less, as for inheritance tax purposes it may qualify as an 'excepted estate'.

9. If the deceased was a beneficiary under a trust or life interest, ask the relevant person what each trust or life interest is, including its value and terms, and if necessary seek legal advice.

10. Start to collect all assets. Fill in forms.

11. Return all forms to the Probate Registry along with the death certificate and any relevant valuations.

12. Confirm date of appointment given to you by the Probate Registry.

13. Arrange finance if necessary to pay for inheritance tax, probate fee.

14. Attend Probate Registry, swear forms, pay probate fee, if necessary pay inheritance tax.

15. Receive grant of probate or letters of administration.

16. If necessary, put a statutory advertisement in local or national papers asking for creditors and other claimants against the estate to reply. Seek legal advice if necessary.

17. If property has been valued by the valuation officer from HM Revenue & Customs, agree the declared value. Additional inheritance tax might have to be paid. Decide with beneficiary of property what he/she would like to happen to it.

18. Complete income tax forms and capital gains tax forms, if necessary, for the period of administration.

19. Apply for and get inheritance tax discharge certificate.

20. Either through loan or through available cash in the estate, pay off any estate liabilities.

21. Pay and transfer any legacies, obtaining receipts.

22. Prepare the final estate accounts with the appropriate tax deduction certificate, R185E, if relevant.

23. If the will provides for life interests or trusts, seek legal advice, as the part of the estate allocated to this will now need transferring over to the trustees if different to yourself.

24. Obtain approval of accounts and receipts from beneficiaries.

25. Distribute assets to beneficiaries or residuary beneficiary and obtain receipts.
26. Write to the bank, closing the bank account.

Probate Fees Payable in England and Wales

Under £5,000	Nil
£5,001 and over	£90 in personal applications
	£40 in solicitors' cases

Fees are charged at the time of application irrespective of the date of death.

Appendix 2
Glossary of Terms

Absolute. Given without any condition. For example, 'I give to … the residue of my estate absolutely' means just that. Whatever is left in the estate is given absolutely over to that named person.

Administrator. A person appointed by the Probate Registry in the absence of a will being found or a person who is appointed by the Registry to prove a will in the event of there being no executor. A relative or close friend of a beneficiary could be asked to administer the estate in order of beneficial priority.

Assets. Your possessions, which, apart from bank accounts, insurance policies, etc, include furniture, cars, jewellery – generally everything.

Beneficiary. A person who inherits (benefits) under a will or under intestacy laws or under a trust.

Bequest. A gift of estate (other than immoveable property such as houses or land).

Bond of caution. According to Scottish law it represents a sum of money which can compensate the estate for any loss caused by an executor's mistake or omission.

Caveat. A legal term or 'caution' giving the Probate Registrar notice that you intend to challenge the specific will. This caution has a life of six months, and it can be renewed. A grant will not be issued when a caveat exists.

Chargeable gift. An item given under the conditions of a will on which tax may have to be paid.

Children. This term now covers both legitimate and illegitimate children, also children who have been legally adopted into the family. It does not include stepchildren. Such persons must therefore be specifically mentioned if they are to benefit under a will. Children who are born as a result of a sperm bank donation have to be specifically named in the will. Mentioning their existence or possible existence without specific title, albeit that instructions are given in the will, could lead to that wish not being fulfilled. At this point, because of the newness of sperm bank donation, this issue is considered to be dangerous, uncharted legal ground and specialist legal advice should be sought.

Codicil. A formal legal document which can be used to make small changes to your will later on. This document operates as part of the originally written will.

Confirmation. The Scottish equivalent of a grant of probate.

Crown. This refers to the Government, whatever department.

Deceased. The person who has died.

Descendants. Any member of your blood line, such as children, grandchildren and so on.

Devise and bequeath. To give a gift under a will or codicil.

Distribution. The process of dealing with an estate after receiving the Grant of Probate or Letters of Administration, first paying debts and then dividing up the remainder between the beneficiaries.

Docket. Scottish term for a formal note.

Donee. A person who receives a gift.

Donor. A person who gives a gift.

Engrossment. Final copy of a legal document.

Excepted estates. This is where an estate gains exemption to supply accounts to HMRC provided certain strict criteria are met, in particular where the net chargeable value of the estate does not exceed £325,000, and consists of property passed under a will or intestacy or nomination or jointly owned passing by survivorship. No more than £100,000 of its value should consist of property outside the United Kingdom and the deceased must have died domiciled in the United Kingdom, having made no lifetime gifts chargeable to either inheritance tax or capital tax or life interests into settlement, but up to £150,000 into a single trust only is acceptable.

Executor. A person appointed by you in your will to deal with the estate. This person cannot charge a fee unless previously authorised by the will, although he or she is able to reclaim out-of-pocket expenses.

Husband. Your spouse who is still alive at the time the will is made (the same definition for **Wife**). In the case of divorce under English law, a couple are still legally married until the decree absolute. For Scottish law, see Chapter 11.

Infant. Now usually referred to as a Minor, in other words a person who is under the age of 18. The law at the moment states that a minor cannot legally hold possessions from an estate until the age of 18. If an asset has been given, then it is given under the terms of a trust to the parent or guardian (known as a trustee) for the benefit of the infant until the age of majority has been reached. You can, if you wish, declare that the minor is to take possession of the legacy before he or she attains his or her age of majority for a specific purpose.

Interest. The right to your property. If total, then it is called *Absolute Interest*.

Intestate. Dying without a will; the rules of intestacy apply – see Chapter 2.

Issue. This means all living descendants.

Joint tenant. This term is applied when two or more people jointly own property and where upon the death of one of them that person's share passes to the surviving joint tenant or tenants. However, the value of the estate that is passed on to the surviving tenant(s) still has to be calculated for inheritance tax purposes. No inheritance tax is payable if the surviving joint tenant is the spouse.

Legacy. A gift of money or property other than house or land.

Legal rights. Under Scottish law this means that the surviving spouse and/or children are entitled, irrespective of the will, to benefit from the estate. Limited rights for a spouse are also now included in English law.

Life interest. The right to enjoy the benefit for life of either money or house or land or, in fact, any property. It reverts to the testator's estate upon the death of the person who enjoyed the life interest, to be received by any person or organisation named as absolute beneficiary.

Life tenant. The person who benefits from a life interest.

Moveable property. This refers to any property other than land or buildings.

Next of kin. Your closest living relative.

Pecuniary legacy. A specific gift of money to a specified person or charity named in your will, eg 'I give £100 to John Brown.'

Personal representative. The person appointed by the Probate Court to deal with your estate in a Grant of Representation. (This would include an executor named by you in your will.)

Power of appointment. The right to nominate persons to receive the benefit of a trust after your death. (Often the person given the power is the present life tenant of the trust.)

Probate. The document issued by the Probate Court which pronounces the validity of a will and upholds the appointment of executor. In Scotland this document is known as *Confirmation*.

Residue. The remainder of an estate after all legacies and bequests have been given to the donees and once all debts, taxes and expenses have been paid.

Small estate. In Scotland it means an estate where the gross value is less than £30,000. This should not be confused with those estates in England and Wales where, because of the small amounts of money involved, ie under £5,000 and termed 'small estates', it is possible to obtain release of the monies in the estate without the legal formality of applying for a grant.

Survivor. Any relative mentioned in the will who is still alive at the time of the testator's death. It also applies to those who may not have been born at the time the will was made but are referred to in it, subject to limitations.

Tenant-in-common. An alternative to joint tenancy for two or more persons to own the same property. In this manner each has a separate share which forms part of his or her estate on death and does not automatically pass to the surviving tenant(s) in common but will pass either under the will or on intestacy.

Testamentary capacity. Essential mental ability needed in order to make a valid will.

Testamentary expenses. The cost of administering a will, eg expenses such as professional fees, telephone, stamps, loss of wages and so on.

Testator. A person who makes a will.

Trust. Parts of an estate (or a whole estate) administered by trustees for the benefit of a named person in accordance with the trust document.

Trustee. A person nominated to deal with a trust.

Appendix 3
Frequently Asked
Questions

If the estate is liable to and pays inheritance tax, but 12 months later when the house and/or shares are sold they are of a lower value than what was declared, can inheritance tax be reclaimed?

Inheritance tax could be reclaimed by applying to Capital Taxes and substituting the original probate value with proof that the sales proceeds were lower and not reinvested in the same company shares or in the repurchase of the house.

What happens if the deceased did not make a will and is a divorcee? Can the former partner make a claim?

If the deceased person was divorced and died intestate, then provided the former spouse has not remarried a claim can be made against the deceased's estate as long as there was no agreement in the divorce proceedings which excluded that person. This does not apply in Scotland.

Do I have to pay for my deceased partner's debts?

Any debts left by the deceased are debts of the deceased person's estate and are settled by the estate before any bequests can be made. Therefore, you as the partner are not liable for your deceased partner's debts unless you have made an agreement whereby you will personally be held liable or you held joint investments. A problem will arise if the deceased person's estate is insolvent. If this should happen then special rules and procedures apply and legal help has to be sought.

How often should I make a new will?

There is no hard and fast rule on exact times – it depends on life-changing events that occur; for example, marriage, birth of a child or children, divorce, death, and so on. You should examine the value of your estate every year or so and certainly consider your will should any of the above changes occur.

Should witnesses read my will before witnessing it?

No, this is not necessary. The witnesses are present to witness your signature, so as long as they have answered for themselves the question that the document being witnessed is *your* will and that you are who you say you are, then that is sufficient.

My grandmother's estate is only valued at £5,000. Do I need to apply for a grant of probate?

In England, Scotland and Wales, this estate value would be termed a small estate. For England and Wales it is possible to obtain a release of monies in an estate without the legal formality of applying for a grant. However, your grandmother's last wishes in her will, if a will has been left, would need to be applied.

The Commissary Office will process small estates under the value of £25,000 provided all details of the estate, assets and debts are supplied.

Both my wife and I made out wills leaving a life interest in our house to our respective spouse. My wife died recently. I wish to sell the house and move to a smaller property. Will I continue to be entitled to the life interest?

Yes, providing the will did not specifically exclude this. You will be entitled to the interest earned on the capital that has been released from the house sale assuming part is needed to purchase the new property. The interest received from the invested capital should be received by you and noted on your Tax Return along with other investment income received.

My father died in 1999 and my mother died in June this year. How does the change in IHT affect my mother's estate?

On the assumption that your mother's estate was over the value of the IHT threshold, and should your father have left his estate to your mother and not previously used the IHT threshold limit gifting it elsewhere in his will, then your mother's executor would be able to apply for the transfer of your late father's unused nil rate band to add to her own. This would have the effect of adding to the threshold before any IHT becomes payable. The transfer has to be applied for and agreed by the Capital Taxes Office before it can be used.

Appendix 4
Useful Addresses

Probate Registries and their local Probate Offices

Birmingham – The Priory Courts, 33 Bull Street, Birmingham B4 6DU. Tel: 0121 681 3400/3414.
Local Probate Offices – Coventry, Kidderminster, Northampton, Wolverhampton.
Bodmin – Market Street, Bodmin PL31 2JW. Tel: 01208 72279.
Local Probate Offices – Plymouth, Truro.
Brighton – William Street, Brighton BN2 2LG. Tel: 01273 573510.
Local Probate Offices – Chichester, Hastings, Horsham.
Bristol – Ground Floor, The Crescent Centre, Temple Back, Bristol BS1 6EP. Tel: 0117 927 3915/926 4619.
Local Probate Offices – Bath, Weston-super-Mare.
Caernarfon – The Criminal Justice Centre, Llanberis Road, Caernarfon LL55 2DF. Tel: 01286 669755
Local Probate Offices – Rhyl, Wrexham.
Cardiff – Probate Registry of Wales, Cardiff Magistrate's Court, 3rd Floor, Fitzalan Place, Cardiff CF24 0RZ. Tel: 02920 474377
Local Probate Offices – Bridgend, Newport, Pontypridd.
Carlisle – Courts of Justice, Earl Street, Carlisle CA1 1DJ. Tel: 01228 521751.

Carmarthen – 14 King Street, Carmarthen SA31 1BL.
Tel: 01267 242560.
Local Probate Offices – Aberystwyth, Haverfordwest, Swansea.
Chester – 5th Floor, Hamilton House, Hamilton Place, Chester
CH1 2DA. Tel: 01244 345082.
Exeter – 1st Floor, Exeter Crown and County Courts,
Southernhay Gardens, Exeter EX1 1UH. Tel: 01392 415370.
Local Probate Offices – Barnstaple, Newton Abbot, Taunton,
Torquay, Yeovil.
Gloucester – 2nd Floor, Combined Court Building, Kimbrose
Way, Gloucester GL1 2DC. Tel: 01452 834966.
Local Probate Offices – Cheltenham, Hereford, Worcester.
Ipswich – Ground Floor, 8 Arcade Street, Ipswich IP1 1EJ.
Tel: 01473 284260.
Local Probate Offices – Chelmsford, Colchester.
Lancaster – Mitre House, Church Street, Lancaster LA1 1HE.
Tel: 01524 36625.
Local Probate Offices – Barrow-in-Furness, Blackpool,
Preston, St Helens.
Leeds – 3rd Floor, Coronet House, Queen Street, Leeds LS1 2BA.
Tel: 0113 386 3540.
Leicester – Crown Court Building, 90 Wellington Street,
Leicester LE1 6HG. Tel: 0116 285 3380.
Local Probate Offices – Bedford.
Lincoln – 360 High Street, Lincoln LN5 7PS. Tel: 01522 523648.
Liverpool – Queen Elizabeth II Law Courts, Derby Square,
Liverpool L2 1XA. Tel: 0151 236 8264.
Local Probate Offices – Southport.
London – Probate Dept, Principal Registry Family Division,
First Avenue House, 42–49 High Holborn, London WC1V 6NP.
Tel: 020 7947 6939.
Local Probate Offices – Croydon, Edmonton, Harlow,
Kingston, Luton, Southend-on-Sea, Woolwich.
Maidstone – The Law Courts, Barker Road, Maidstone
ME16 8EQ. Tel: 01622 202048.
Local Probate Offices – Canterbury, Tunbridge Wells.

Manchester – Manchester Civil Justice Centre, Ground Floor, 1 Bridge Street West, PO Box 4240, Manchester M60 1WJ. Tel: 0161 240 5700.
Local Probate Offices – Bolton, Nelson, Oldham, Warrington, Wigan.
Middlesbrough – Combined Court Centre, Russell Street, Middlesbrough TS1 2AE. Contact Newcastle DPR for opening hours.
Newcastle upon Tyne – No 1 Waterloo Square, Newcastle upon Tyne NE1 4AL. Tel: 0191 211 2170.
Local Probate Offices – Darlington.
Norwich – Combined Court Building, The Law Courts, Bishopgate, Norwich NR3 1UR. Tel: 01603 728267.
Local Probate Offices – King's Lynn, Lowestoft.
Nottingham – Butt Dyke House, 33 Park Row, Nottingham NG1 6GR. Tel: 0115 941 4288.
Oxford – Combined Court Building, St Aldates, Oxford OX1 1LY. Tel: 01865 793055.
Local Probate Offices – Aylesbury, High Wycombe, Reading, Slough, Swindon.
Peterborough – 1st Floor, Crown Buildings, Rivergate, Peterborough PE1 1EJ. Tel: 01733 562802.
Local Probate Offices – Cambridge.
Sheffield – PO Box 832, The Law Courts, 50 West Bar, Sheffield S3 8YR. Tel: 0114 281 2596.
Stoke-on-Trent – Combined Court Centre, Bethesda Street, Hanley, Stoke-on-Trent ST1 3BP. Tel: 01782 854065.
Local Probate Offices – Crewe, Shrewsbury, Stafford.
Winchester – 4th Floor, Cromwell House, Andover Road, Winchester SO23 7EW. Tel: 01962 897029.
Local Probate Offices – Basingstoke, Bournemouth, Dorchester, Guildford, Newport (Isle of Wight), Portsmouth, Salisbury, Southampton.
York – 1st Floor, Castle Chambers, Clifford Street, York YO1 9RG. Tel: 01904 666777.
Local Probate Offices – Hull, Scarborough.

Useful addresses in Scotland

Registrar of Deeds
Registers of Scotland
Meadowbank House
153 London Road
Edinburgh EH8 7AU
(0131 659 6111)

HM Commissary Office
27 Chambers Street
Edinburgh EH1 1LB
(0131 225 2525)
www.scotcourts.gov.uk

Supplier of inheritance tax inventory forms
Capital Taxes Office
Meldrum House
15 Drumsheugh Gardens
Edinburgh EH3 7UG
(0131 777 4050)

Forms can also be obtained from main post offices throughout
Scotland.

Pensions

The www.pensionservice.gov.uk (0845 600 2537).

Insurance

Association of British Insurers (020 7600 3333)
www.abi.org.uk.

Unit Trusts and Investment Trusts

Investment Management Association for Unit Trusts (020 7831
0898) www.investmentfunds.org.uk.

Appendix 5
Tax Thresholds and Allowances 2009/10

Inheritance tax   £325,000
Death rate of tax over this   40 per cent
Lifetime rate of tax   20 per cent

Capital Gains Tax general exemption limit individual £10,100
standard rate 18 per cent

Trusts and personal representatives £5,050 (gains taxed at
40 per cent)

Entrepreneurs relief on part or whole disposal of a business;
first £1 million of gain at effective rate of 10 per cent. Gain
on remainder taxed at 18 per cent.

Income tax rates

After personal allowance or personal age related allowance,
whichever is applicable:

Up to £37,400 at 20 per cent
From £37,401 plus 40 per cent

Income tax reliefs

Personal allowance

Age under 65   £6,475
Age 65–74   £9,490
Age 75 and over   £9,640

Age allowance reduced by £1 for every £2 over minimum where limit exceeds £22,900 and basic under 65 allowance applied thereafter.

Married couple's allowance (restricted to 10 per cent relief)

Under 75 and born after 6 April 1935   NIL
Either spouse 75 or over   £6,965

Index

NB: page numbers in *italic* indicate tables

Index of Advertisers